Y0-DNG-119

A Visitor's Guide to
THE SCOTTISH BORDERS
AND EDINBURGH

EDINBURGH

KEY FOR MAPS

Towns - Villages
Main Roads
County Boundary
Rivers
Railways
Lakes/Reservoirs

Museum/Art
Gallery/Centre

Archaeological Site

Building/
Country Park
Gardens

Castle/Fort

Ecclesiastical
Building

Other Place
of Interest

Visitor's Guide Series

This series of guide books gives, in each volume, the details and facts needed to make the most of a holiday in one of the tourist areas of Britain and Europe. Not only does the text describe the countryside, villages, and towns of each region, but there is also valuable information on where to go and what there is to see. Each book includes, where appropriate, stately homes, gardens and museums to visit, nature trails, archaeological sites, sporting events, steam railways, cycling, walking, sailing, fishing, country parks, useful addresses — everything to make your visit more worthwhile.

Other titles already published or planned include:
The Lake District (Revised Edition)
The Peak District
The Chilterns
The Cotswolds
North Wales
The Yorkshire Dales
Cornwall
Devon
Somerset and Dorset
Dordogne (France)
Guernsey, Alderney and Sark

A Visitor's Guide To
THE SCOTTISH BORDERS AND EDINBURGH

Roger Smith

MOORLAND PUBLISHING

Illustrations were provided by:
Richard Wilson p 41; Roger Smith p 37; The
Scottish Tourist Board p 26 (upper and lower),
27-8, 32-3, 34, 36, 39 (upper and lower), 46, 48-
9, 53, 56, 59, 61, 62-3 (upper and lower), 65, 70,
81, 83, 91, 94, 96-7; Scottish Field p 15, 16, 18,
22, 44-5, 47, 69, 75, 79, 85, 88-9, 93, 96 (inset);
City of Edinburgh Public Relations Dept.p 99,
101, 104-5, 106, 108-9.

© Roger Smith 1983

ISBN 0 86190 086 3 (hardback)
ISBN 0 86190 087 1 (paperback)

All rights reserved. No part of this publication may be reproduced, stored in a
retrieval system, or transmitted in any
form or by any means, electronic, mech-
anical, photocopying, recording or otherwise, without prior permission of Moorland Publishing Company Ltd.

Printed in the UK by
Butler and Tanner Ltd, Frome
for the publishers
Moorland Publishing Co Ltd,
9-11 Station Street, Ashbourne,
Derbyshire, DE6 1DE England.
Telephone: (0335) 44486

British Library Cataloguing
in Publication Data

Smith, Roger, 1938-
    A Visitor's Guide to the Scottish
    Border and Edinburgh.
    1. Scotland — Description and travel
    — 1981 — Guide-books
    I. Title
    914.11'04858   DA870

Contents

1 Introduction -The Borders

The first problem confronting anyone writing a book about the Scottish Borders is to define the area. We all recognise that there is an area known as 'The Borders' but where does it begin and end?

On the south and east sides there is little difficulty. The Border itself forms the southern boundary, running from Berwick-on-Tweed (which I have included as, although it is administratively in England, it seems to me to be absolutely a Borders town) west and southwards to the wide expanse of the Solway Firth. The eastern boundary is the Berwickshire coast, which stretches as far north as Cockburnspath.

When you turn inland from there, the problems start. There has been, since 1974, an administrative region called 'Borders' but its northern and western edges did not seem to me to define the area I wished to cover. I took the dilemma to Alf Scott, then Tourism Officer for the Regional Council, and have happily adopted the common-sense solution he suggested.

The northern edge of the area covered in this book more or less follows the 200-metre shading contour on the Bartholomew's 1:100,000 National Series maps, except where lower ground is actually in Borders Region. This avoids the rather unnatural boundary of the region, which runs higher on the hills. The exception is the piece of land in the Pentland Hills around West Linton. It seemed to me that with the Pentlands it was a case of all in or not at all; as I don't class them as Border hills, I have left them out.

Our border therefore runs south-westwards down the A701 and A72 from Leadburn to Biggar, and then along A702 to Abington. From here, I have followed the A74 — the artery that takes so many people through the Borders without stopping, sadly — down to Gretna. I believe this gives us a cohesive area which can truly be described as 'the Scottish Borders'.

What are its characteristics? Much of it is hill land, the Border itself reaching 722m (2,382ft) at Auchope Cairn. The main hill ranges run south-west to north-east, and are named Tweedsmuir, Moorfoot and Lammermuir in that order. There is very little in the way of dramatic rock architecture, nearly all the hills being rounded and well grassed, which makes them excellent walking country.

The hills are riven by glorious river valleys which give superlative fishing and have provided the base for a flourishing textile industry. The best-known of these rivers, again west to east and working northwards as well, are the Liddel, Teviot, Ettrick, Moffat, Yarrow, and the Tweed, which forms the actual boundary between Scotland and England in its lower reaches.

Along these river valleys are attractive Border towns such as Hawick, Kelso, Selkirk and Peebles. They all form excellent bases for a touring holiday and within easy reach of any of them you will find opportunities for exploration, recreation and education in the form of castles, historic houses, and museums.

The south-east of the region is generally lower-lying and more intensively farmed. The rich lands of

Berwickshire reach right to the coast, which itself is studded with gems: fishing villages tucked into natural harbours, clifftop castles, beaches and birdlife (there is a major wildlife reserve at St Abb's Head).

The Border region has been fought over since pre-Roman times, as is evidenced by the several hilltop forts still clearly to be seen. There are two in the area of the Eildon Hills, near Melrose.

The Romans knew the Borders well, as an area of wild country between their two major northern lines of defence, the walls attributed to Hadrian (from the Solway Firth to the Northumberland coast) and to Antoninus (across the waist of Scotland from Dumbarton on the Clyde to the Forth estuary). They too chose the Eildon Hills for a

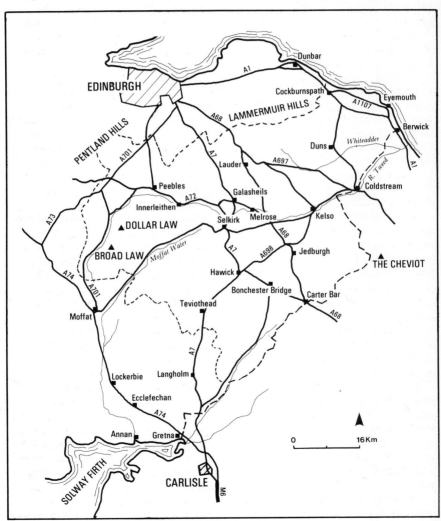

stronghold, *Trimontium*.

In the Middle Ages the Border itself shifted back and forth a number of times until it was settled more or less along its present line, first by the Laws of the Marches in 1249 and then by the Treaty of Northampton (actually signed in Edinburgh) in 1325. That was not, of course, the end of the fighting. Far from it, as you will find in all the Border towns and in their museums.

Perhaps the most tragic battle of all was one of the last; the debacle of Flodden, in 1513, when so many noble Scots fell. It was this battle that gave rise to the moving pipe lament 'The Flowers of the Forest'.

Battles today are more likely to be political than physical, and there is certainly far less 'reiving' (rustling of cattle and sheep by daring raids). None the less, the border is decidedly a place of change. I can never cross it, either way, even on the roaring maelstrom of the A74, without being aware that I am passing between two very different lands. At the highest and most dramatic main road crossing, Carter Bar, is the site of another battle, in 1575, and despite the teabar and tourist information boards it is still a place where an uneasy glance over the shoulder comes naturally.

Having mentioned Carter Bar and the A74, let us go on and consider access and transport in more detail. The old ways that cross the region — the Roman Dere Street and the drove roads — now make splendid walking routes, and a number of them are described later in this book. For today's visitor, the M6 and A74 give easy access from the south, and can be left either by the A7 up to Hawick or by the A708 Moffat/Selkirk road.

The A68 will take you from Newcastle over Carter Bar to Jedburgh in well under two hours. It is my favoured approach unless I am really in a hurry. A little further east, the A697 winds up through Wooler to cross the Tweed into Scotland at historic Coldstream, and on the east coast the A1 — the Great North Road itself — takes a longer but very beautiful route, keeping close to the sea all the way.

There are main rail lines to west and east still; I regret the passing of the smaller Border lines but they are gone, no doubt for ever. The western line carries regular services from Glasgow down through Carlisle, and the east coast has the express Edinburgh-London route. There are very few stopping points of use to the Borders visitor; without a car it is best to alight at either Berwick, Carlisle or Edinburgh and use buses to penetrate from there.

Border buses still provide a good network, and an excellent comprehensive timetable is available. It repays a bit of careful study to maximise connections. The area, finally, is ideally suited to the slower means of travel — cycling and walking. Apart from the few trunk routes, the roads are generally quiet, and great for touring cyclists. Inexpensive accommodation with a friendly welcome is not hard to find, and there is no shortage either of refreshment places or distractions calling for a stop during the day's pedalling.

Accommodation generally is unlikely to be a problem to the Borders visitor. All grades can be found from good hotels with excellent cuisine to the many comfortable bed-and-breakfast houses. Wherever you stay, the welcome will be warm and you will be well looked after.

There are a number of self-catering schemes in the region, offering either cottages or caravans, and there are youth hostels at Kirk Yetholm, Ferniehirst, Snoot (near Hawick), Melrose, Broadmeadows (near Selkirk) and Coldingham on the coast. See Further Information for details. Broadmeadows is a piece of history; it was the first hostel opened by the SYHA in 1931 and has been going strong ever since.

Information about accommodation can either be had in advance, using one of the several excellent guides available, or locally at a Tourist Information Centre. These are to be found at all main centres of population, and a list is given in Further Information.

Some of these information centres operate a 'book-a-bed-ahead' service, through which you can secure accommodation in the price range of your choice for a small fee. This is a useful service but it is not essential in the Borders — a reflection of the fact that the area could do with more visitors. I hope this book will help.

What about recreation? For the active Borders visitor, there is plenty of choice. The walking, of course, is first-class, whether your taste is for coastlines or high hills. A new waymarked long-distance route, the Southern Uplands Way, is due to be opened in 1984. It will stretch from Portpatrick near Stranraer to St Abb's Head on the Berwickshire coast. Suggestions for shorter walks are given in the text.

The Borders Regional Council countryside rangers operate a programme of guided walks in the summer months, and several hotels cater specially for the walker. The youth hostel network is also an ideal framework for a walking (or cycling) holiday.

Pony-trekking thrives; the Border hills and quiet byways are absolutely ideal for travel on horseback, and a leaflet on the subject can be obtained from the Regional Tourist Board or from the Scottish Tourist Board. All classes and ages are catered for.

Another principal recreation is, not surprisingly, fishing. The Tweed and its tributaries are famous game fishing waters, not least because the entire water system is free from any industrial pollution. No fewer than sixteen different species of fish were noted in a recent survey!

The salmon season runs from the beginning of February to late November and in the autumn run, fish of around 20-25lb weight are not unusual. Most of the better beats are not unnaturally in private hands, but there are several places where the visitor can try his luck — perhaps notably on the Tweed in Peebles. The brown trout season on the Tweed is limited to between 1 April and 30 September, and the area is unusual in that a Trout Protection Order was introduced in 1980.

Under this Order, it is an offence to fish for brown trout anywhere in the Scottish section of the Tweed watershed without having a permit, or the express permission of the owner of the water. Don't despair — all tackle shops in the area issue permits at very reasonable rates and are only too glad to help visitors with information. Some hotels own the rights to particular stretches of water, too.

For the angler who prefers still water, there are plenty of places to choose from — larger lochs such as St Mary's, and smaller areas of water, notably around Hawick. The fishing is mostly for trout, but Alemoor and Hellmoor Lochs contain specimen pike and perch. Sea and coarse fishermen can also follow their chosen sport in the Borders. Eyemouth has a thriving Sea Angling Club, and is well known for its excellent rock fishing. The coarse fisherman is well catered for on the lower reaches of Tweed and Teviot. There are roach, dace and perch in the Tweed, and grayling in the Teviot.

There is no close season for coarse fishing in Scotland, but some areas on the Tweed operate restrictions at certain times to protect salmon and trout stocks. Full information is available locally or via the Regional Tourist Board.

There are six full 18-hole golf courses in the region — at Galashiels, Hawick, Kelso, Minto, Peebles and West Linton — and a further eleven 9-hole courses. Many of these are delightfully scenic and all of them welcome visitors. Some hotels, such as the Peebles Hydro, arrange special Golf Weeks.

Other recreational possibilities include sailing on St Mary's Loch and off the Berwickshire coast, and orienteering at any one of several permanent courses operated by the Forestry Commission in conjunction with local clubs.

If your taste is for a less strenuous holiday, the choice is just as wide. One of the great features of the region is the series of Common Ridings and Festivals held at all principal towns. There are twelve main ridings and celebrations, running more or less one a week from early June to mid-August. They have their origins in the need to define and protect common land and many of them celebrate historical incidents. All are colourful spectacles and although they are celebrations for the local community, they are also prime attractions for visitors.

The round begins in the west, at West Linton in fact, where the Whipman is chosen at the beginning of June. Around the same time, the first of several Cornets, at Hawick, makes his appearance. The Cornet is a bachelor of the town and is supported by his Left Hand and Right Hand Man, the two previous Cornets.

Hawick's ceremonies are largely all-male affairs, the Cornet's Lass making one of her few appearances when she 'busses' the burgh flag by tying blue and gold ribbons to the flagpole. The Cornet's Walk then takes all the principals to the 'Horse' monument where he performs a similar bussing, commemorating the battle of Hornshole in 1514. Ridings and other events go on for five weeks.

Next in line is Selkirk, where the riding has its origin in the battle of Flodden. The principal is here called the Standard Bearer and the two main events are the Riding of the Marches, and the Casting of the Flag in Selkirk Market Place.

Melrose's man is called simply The Melrosian and he has, as his Festival Queen, the Dux Girl of Melrose Grammar School. The Rideout covers the Eildon Hills and Gattonside Heights and festival events follow for a week.

The Beltane Festival in Peebles is another colourful affair, with another Cornet, Cornet's Lass, and a Beltane Queen, a young lady from the primary school. There is a grand procession round the town, with several hundred children on floats, riding of the Marches, and horse racing on the golf course.

The Braw Lads Gathering in Galashiels started in 1830, and not surprisingly the principals are the Braw Lad and Braw Lass. There are several Rides, the main one being on a Saturday when the Braw Lad receives the burgh flag, and fords the Tweed on horseback to visit the house of Abbotsford, where the party is received by the descendants of Sir Walter Scott.

Duns Summer Festival takes place during the first full week in July and its principals are the Reiver and his Lass, and the Wynsome Maid o'Dunse, who is crowned in the public park. Rideouts visit Duns Law and Duns Castle, and towards the end of the week the ancient game of handba' takes place — the married men versus the bachelors, and no holds barred!

Jedburgh has one of the longest Rideouts — all the way to the border itself at Redeswire, site of the battle in 1575 where Jedburgh men helped to defeat the English. The burgh flag is carried by the Callant, and there are other rides to Lanton and Ferniehirst Castle. The week ends with the Jedburgh Games.

The Kelso Laddie leads the parade during Civic Week in the town, and his rides take him and his supporters to Roxburgh, Ednam, Floors Castle, and to Yetholm. The riding at Langholm is a true marking of the ancient boundaries, and is always held on the last Friday in July. A unique feature is that the colours worn by the Cornet are those of the winner of the Epsom Derby! Another oddity is that the Cornet is elected by a ballot in which anyone over 15 can vote — even non-residents and visitors.

Not to be missed is the town ride in which the mounted party gallop up the steep Kirkwynd, and by Whitta Yett to Castle Craigs. The cavalcade is met by a procession of children all carrying heather besoms, and the horsemen ford the River Ewes to Castleholm, where the Cornet's Chase is run.

Lauder Common Riding was revived in 1910 to mark the coronation of King George V, and has been held ever since, on the first Saturday in August. At the Burgess Cairn, the only remaining boundary stone, the Cornet adds a small stone before leading the return to Lauder. In the afternoon there are sports and gymkhana events.

The final festival is celebrated at Coldstream, on the very border between Scotland and England. The main ride goes into England, to Flodden Field itself, where the Coldstreamer (a young man under 30) lays a wreath at the memorial. An oration is given by an invited speaker.

Another ride goes to The Hirsel, home of Lord Home, who as Sir Alec Douglas-Home was Prime Minister. Among the week's other activities is an 'exiles' tea', a very popular event bringing Coldstreamers of all ages together.

Apart from these annual events, other festivals with specific themes such as fishing, golf or Borders life are arranged by the regional or district councils each year. Details can be found in the guides listed in the Further Information.

Weather is an important consideration for any visitor, so what can you expect in the Borders? The eastern part of the region is generally drier than the west, as is true for the whole of Scotland — the western hills catch the rain borne on the prevailing south-westerly winds first. On the other hand, the west is a little warmer overall than the east. Scotland's east coast, including Berwickshire, has some glorious sandy beaches, but it does suffer from rather too much east wind, and also on occasion from 'haar' — a sea fog that can blanket the coast in a cold mist while 20 miles inland is glorious sunshine.

The Berwickshire coast is, however, still among the sunniest places in Scotland from May to July, recording an average 6-6½ hours per day of bright sunshine. These (particularly May and early June) are the months when good settled spells are most likely; the spring is my personal favourite among seasons, with the trees in fresh leaf and summer birds arriving.

Records taken over the whole holiday period from May to September show that eastern areas of Scotland often record less than 250mm (10in) of rain during this time; so you will be unlucky if you get a long spell of wet weather. Showers can never be ruled out, of course, but the scenery is often at its most dramatic and rewarding in these conditions, with the quality of the light constantly changing — a challenge for the photographer.

The autumn period can also have advantages. The weather is quite often dry, there are fewer visitors overall — so that roads are less crowded, and the trees are in brilliant colouring along the river valleys. The air on the hills is invigorating, and a walking holiday in the Borders in September or October could have much to commend it.

Extremes of temperature are rare in the region, though I have to say that, when we lived in Peebles, we experienced several nights at -20°C in winter. The weather station at Eskdalemuir, in the west of the region, also holds the unenviable record of the most concentrated period of rain ever recorded in Scotland — $3\frac{1}{2}$inches in one hour, on 26 June 1953.

One blessing is that the region is much less prone to the irritations of the midge than more northerly parts of Scotland. This little pest can be a real menace in summer in the western highlands, but you are unlikely to suffer too badly in the Borders.

The Borders Region today has a population of just on 100,000 — which gives plenty of space for everyone. I have always found it a welcoming region, with no shortage of things to see and do, and no shortage either of glorious countryside to wander in or ride through. I hope this book will give a broad picture of what is available and will tempt you to try for yourself this often neglected part of Scotland.

I have not yet described the whole area covered by the book. As you will have seen, it is a guide to the Scottish Borders — and Edinburgh. Edinburgh is such a major attraction for visitors to Scotland, and is so easily accessible from the Border, that it made sense to include it in this guide. It has a chapter to itself at the end.

A mere chapter, when so many full books have been written about Edinburgh, may seem almost to be an insult. It is not meant to be. It is meant as a taster, a sample of some of the things Scotland's capital has to offer. Edinburgh is many different cities packed into one — Auld Reekie, the Athens of the North, the Festival City, it is all these and more. It has a royal home and many fascinating relics of the life of ordinary people in days gone by.

At any time of year, Edinburgh will occupy your mind and body for as long as you wish. It is a centre of the arts, and has a mini-wilderness in its centre where you can wander free and study birdlife. It has smart restaurants and downbeat cafes and bistros. In August and early September it goes slightly mad when the great International Festival — particularly the Fringe, which is now bigger than the main event — takes over.

Don't try to know Edinburgh from my one chapter. Go there for yourself. But before doing so, be fair to the Borders and stay awhile in this most rewarding region of Scotland — you won't regret doing so!

2 The Border and the Cheviot Hills

You could perhaps define a border as a historical accident that has become historical fact. Most people would express surprise that there could be any doubt as to the line of the border between Scotland and England; but, given a map without the border on it and asked to draw it in, nearly everyone gets it wrong. Try it yourself and see!

The border as now defined makes

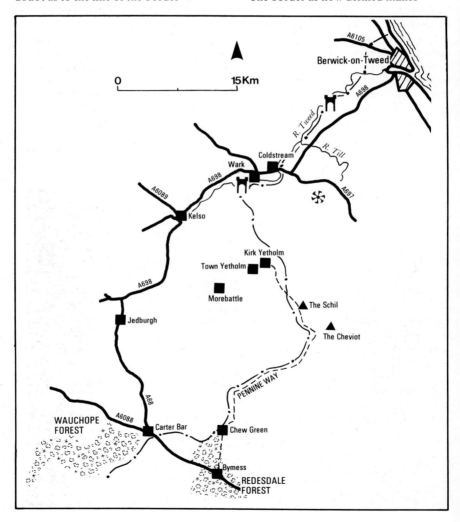

some odd-looking twists and turns, at one point heading south-east when its basic alignment is south-west to north-east. Let us start on the east coast and trace the border across, at the same time having a look at the land and places immediately to either side of it.

The first surprise is that Berwick-on-Tweed is not in Scotland, but in England. By all that's reasonable, it should be a Scottish town. It sits on the north bank of the Tweed, and should surely belong to Berwick*shire* — indeed, most people would assume that it is the county town! Not so; Berwick is firmly in Northumberland, England, despite being a burgh not a borough. How did this come about?

In the fifteenth century, Berwick was one of the four royal burghs of Scotland.

In 1482, King James III of Scotland, a rather weak monarch, fell out with his brother, the Duke of Albany, who turned to the English king, Edward IV, for help. Seeing a chance to do himself a bit of good, Edward lent Albany an army under the charge of his own brother (who was to become Richard III), the plan being to overthrow James and install Albany on the Scottish throne as a liege of Edward's.

In fact, Edward was really more interested in acquiring Berwick, a strategic port and trading point of great importance. The invasion duly took place, but Richard had no real intention of engaging in a full-scale war with the Scots. At Haddington, east of Edinburgh, he gave way to James's army with the minimum of losses to his own

The three bridges of Berwick-on-Tweed

force. The price he demanded for withdrawing his troops was the secession of Berwick. James agreed, and despite many subsequent attempts to right the wrong, Berwick has stayed as a part of English soil ever since.

None the less, it would be unusual for anyone to pass over the Tweed there without the definite feeling of crossing a b)rder; not least because of the manner of the crossing. Bridges have always been important to Berwick. There was a timber bridge here for centuries before the oldest structure still standing; the James VI bridge was built in the early years of the seventeenth century. For its time, it is a marvellous piece of work, with fifteen arches and a total span of 1,164ft — nearly 400 yards of river!

No less spectacular, and certainly more obvious to the modern traveller, is the Royal Border Bridge which carries the railway into the town. Designed by Robert Stephenson, son of George of *Rocket* fame, it has no fewer than twenty-five tall arches, spans just over 2,000 feet and was opened by Queen Victoria in 1850. You get an excellent view of it from the third Berwick bridge, carrying the A1 road. This is a mere youngster; it was completed in 1928, and reflects modern engineering design in that the number of arches has been reduced to three.

A feature of Berwick is the impressive Town Wall, one of the most complete in Britain. It encloses the old town and gives a real impression of a fortified burgh if you walk round it.

A town that has seen so many battles should have a castle; and so it has, even though it is not such an impressive

Part of the ancient walls of Berwick

affair. The railway is partly to blame for that, for when Berwick station was built in the nineteenth century, a goodly chunk of the castle ruins were cleared to make way for the iron horse. Enough remains to impress on the visitor the strength of its position, on a high bluff above the river. From 1306 to 1310, Isobel, Countess of Buchan, was suspended outside the castle walls in an iron cage, by the command of Edward I, because she had fulfilled her duty by placing the Scottish crown on the head of Robert the Bruce. She survived, as did Bruce's sister Mary, hung similarly outside Roxburgh Castle.

The border line meets the coast three miles north of Berwick and describes a swinging loop to the west of the town, meeting the Tweed at Gainslaw. After this, there is no more nonsense for a while, river and border running together as far as Carham, west of Coldstream. This is all low-lying, rich, agricultural land, though the hills are never out of sight completely. On the Scottish side, the area is called the Merse, and is covered more fully in the chapter on Berwickshire. The principal type of agriculture is arable farming for cereals, with a good amount of malting barley produced for both beer and whisky production. Fruit and vegetables have become more popular in recent years.

After Berwick, the next river crossing point is the Union Bridge at Horncliffe, best approached by a minor road from the A698. It is worth going to see, for this was the first suspension bridge in Britain to carry vehicular traffic when it was opened in 1820. It was designed by Captain Sir Samuel Brown and was opened as a toll-bridge. The tollhouse, on the English side, was demolished in 1955 and replaced by a small forecourt made up of the cottage's foundations. The bridge is listed as an Ancient Monument.

With the Union and Coldstream bridges, Norham Bridge is administered by the Tweed Bridges Trust. The Trust was formed in 1884, at the time when Norham became the third 'border bridge' over the Tweed, replacing an older timber structure. It carries B6470 across the river to Ladykirk. The church here was built in the late fifteenth century at the order of James IV of Scotland as a thank-offering for a narrow escape from drowning in the Tweed. It was built entirely of stone to avoid the risk of fire, presumably with those Border raiders in mind!

Fifteen miles from Berwick, and still on the Tweed, is the first true Border town, Coldstream. Before the border reaches there, however, the Tweed has been joined by the Till, crossed by the Tudor bridge at Twizel. A famous rhyme underlines the truth of the saying that 'still waters run deep':

> Tweed said to Till,
> What gars ye rin sae still?
> Till said tae Tweed,
> Though ye rin wi' speed,
> and I rin slaw,
> Whaur ye droun ae man,
> I droun twa'.

So to Coldstream, and the third of the Tweed Border Bridges. Coldstream Bridge was built by John Smeaton (who gained more fame as a lighthouse-builder), and completed in 1766 at a cost of £6,000. The small stone building on the Scottish side of the bridge, built as a tollhouse, became far better known as a marriage-house which rivalled the one at Gretna in popularity. The practice was stopped by an Act of Parliament in 1856. Downstream of the bridge is a small dam or 'cauld' with a gap at its south end to allow fish free run.

At the entrance to the main street is

PLACES TO VISIT AROUND COLDSTREAM

Guards Museum, Coldstream
Exhibits showing the history of the regiment.

The Dovecot, Coldstream
Eighteenth-century bird loft.

The Hirsel, off A697 1m west of Coldstream
Home of Lord Home. Grounds open — wild fowl sanctuary, nature trails, visitor centre.

Flodden Field
Site of battle in 1513.

Wark Castle
Border ruin which saw the origin of the Order of the Garter.

Kirk Yetholm
Northern end of Pennine Way footpath. Former gipsy stronghold.

Bridge over the Tweed at Coldstream

the monument to Charles Marjoribanks, first MP for Berwickshire after the Reform Act of 1832.Off Market Square, near the river, is the Coldstream Guards Museum. The original company of Guards was raised in this area by General Monck in 1659; they marched to London in thirty-four days and helped to restore order and the monarchy, following the death of Oliver Cromwell. The close association between Guards and town has been maintained ever since; the museum houses many exhibits illustrating the history of the regiment, and also the scroll commemorating the occasion in August 1968 when the regiment was honoured with the Freedom of the Burgh. The colours of

the 2nd Battalion are laid up in the parish church, together with a side drum and a bugle.

Another interesting old building is The Dovecot, facing the Leet Water. It dates from the late eighteenth century. Penitents' Walk, which runs along the Leet to the Tweed, and Nuns' Walk which joins it, are reminders that there was once a Cistercian Priory here. Nothing remains but these two names.

If you take the walk, you are likely to see fishermen trying their luck; if you wish to join them, you will be welcome to do so in season. Visitors' permits for trout and coarse fishing are available locally at very reasonable rates. Enquire at the Tourist Information Centre at Henderson Park. Other facilities for visitors include a caravan and camp site nicely sited by the river and more than adequate hotel and guest house accommodation.

A couple of miles from Coldstream, off the A697, is The Hirsel, the seat of the Home family and presently the home of Lord Home, the former Prime Minister. The house itself is not open to the public, but the grounds are open all the year round. There is a wild fowl sanctuary and a very wide variety of birdlife in the splendid woods. Nature trails are laid out, and the estate interpretation centre will be glad to give visitors further details. Flower displays of particular interest include daffodils in April and rhododendrons in June.

Whilst in the Coldstream area, a short excursion into England will give a fuller picture of Border history. No visitor to the area should leave without a trip to Flodden Field, where the site of the battle is marked by a simple stone cross. Flodden has been described as 'the worst defeat ever inflicted on a Scots army', the general responsible being the Earl of Surrey. After the battle was over, on that sad day in 1513, the bodies were piled up in Branxton churchyard, some of them later being buried by the nuns at Coldstream. Among the 5,000 dead was James IV, King of Scotland, and the slaughter inspired Jane Elliot to write the words which in turn inspired the fine pipe lament: 'The flowers of the forest are all we'ed away'.

A little way west of Coldstream, on the English bank of the river, is Wark, where a mighty castle once stood. This place was the origin of the Order of the Garter, which really did begin as you might imagine. Edward III was staying in the castle and during a ball, he was dancing with the lady of the house, the Countess of Salisbury, when one of her garters came loose and fell upon the floor. Edward picked it up and checked the assembly's mirth by saying with dignity 'honi soit qui mal y pense' — the words chosen as the motto of the noble Order.

Four miles west of Coldstream, the border takes an abrupt turn south-east, away from Tweed and as if drawn by magnetism to the high Cheviot Hills. At the point where it turns, Birgham, a treaty was signed in 1290, reaffirming the independence of the Scots. Echoes of it still resound today, though fortunately the impulse to raise an army and raid the English has died!

The border crosses the valley of the Bowmont Water before climbing Coldsmouth Hill and linking the summits of White Law, Black Hag, The Schil, and Auchope Cairn, at 2,382ft its highest point. Bowmont Water divides the twin villages of Town Yetholm and Kirk Yetholm, which in earlier times were gipsy strongholds. The last Queen of the Gipsies, Esther Faa Blythe, died in 1883. There is a nature reserve run by the Scottish Wildlife Trust at Yetholm Loch, but access is by permit only.

No permits are needed to walk the Pennine Way, which was the first designated long distance footpath in Britain. Most people walk it south to north, starting at Edale in the Peak District National Park, and so finishing their 250-mile journey at Kirk Yetholm. Their first port of call is frequently the Border Hotel, where a free celebratory drink, courtesy of the guidebook writer A. Wainwright, has been the custom since the path opened. Originally, you got a pint on Mr Wainwright, but so many people now walk the route that the bounty has been reduced to a half. There are only two conditions — you must have walked the whole route, and you must be carrying Wainwright's *Pennine Way Companion* when you enter the pub. So, one way and another, you don't really get your drink for nothing . . . .

Using the Wainwright guidebook, with its superb maps and line drawings, or any other similarly detailed guide, you can reverse the modern pilgrims' triumphant finish, and walk southwards from Kirk Yetholm towards the border. It's a splendid outing, however far you go; over the hill and up the valley to Burnhead, then round the slopes of The Curr and up again to meet the border on The Schil, with Cheviot itself looming up to the south-east. To The Schil and back is about twelve miles, but you can retrace your steps at any point and still have a most enjoyable walk.

This last stage of the Pennine Way is generally reckoned to be the toughest, if you are trying to do it in one day. The last previous habitation is at Byrness, and the path follows the border all the way from Coquet Head to The Schil. The full distance from Byrness to Kirk Yetholm is not much short of thirty miles, with a goodly amount of climbing and some rough and boggy ground to traverse.

If you prefer being carried by four sturdy legs rather than using your own two, there is a trekking centre at Belford, high in the Bowmont Valley. Beginners are catered for, and the proprietors will also advise on walks in the area.

The border line stays almost on the watershed all the way along this stretch, now running south-westwards. It passes the dramatic gash of the Hen Hole on its way to within a mile of Cheviot summit — a diversion most Pennine Wayfarers seem to take, despite its being one of the most notoriously nasty bits of peat bog in Britain. For those for whom the struggle becomes a bit too much and Kirk Yetholm is just out of reach, there is a shelter (an old railway wagon) on the slopes of Cheviot which can be used as an emergency bothy.

The hills are crossed by a number of tracks and droving routes and, further south-west by Coquet Head, by the Roman Road named Dere Street, which leaves the impressive site of the camp at Chew Green heading north towards Kelso. Dere Street can be followed for many miles by the dedicated walker, though access from public roads is not easy. Just on the Scottish side of the border, and just east of Dere Street, is the fort on Woden Law, a pre-Roman stronghold that was overrun by Agricola's army in AD80. The Romans took it over, enlarged it, and (it is believed) used it for training purposes.

Just on the English side, by Coquet Head, and on the Pennine Way, is Chew Green, an impressive Roman camp and an important staging-post on Dere Street. So, with a northwards twist, the Border reaches its highest main road crossing at Carter Bar. At over 1,300 feet, it makes a dramatic entry point into Scotland for any traveller. As you crest the rise after the long climb from Catcleugh Reservoir, a great panorama of hills unfolds before you, with the triple peaks of Eildon prominent. In the summer months, there is a tourist information point, a tea-bar, and often the almost obligatory lone piper here to mark your crossing.

From Carter Bar the line heads due south-west again, over Carter Fell and through the vast coniferous spread of Kielder Forest, one of the largest man-made forests in Europe. With the construction of Kielder Water, opened in 1982 by Her Majesty the Queen, a wide range of recreational possibilities has been opened up in Kielder. On the Scottish side the forest is called Wauchope. This is all part of the Border Forest Park, but there are no formalised recreations in Wauchope.

The next place where a motorable road crosses the Border is the grimly-named Deadwater. It is on the line of another Roman road, the Wheel Causeway. Deadwater is a true watershed — within half a mile of it you will find the Deadwater Burn, which runs into

Kielder Water, and thus to the Tyne and the North Sea, and Liddel Water, which runs down the beautiful Liddesdale to the Esk and so to the Solway Firth. Confounding Kipling, this is one place where east and west do meet.

The Border line runs with Kershope Burn through another large area of forest, now with Cumbria to the south, to join Liddel Water at Kershopefoot. It stays with Liddel until that river joins

the Esk. We are out of the hills now, on to less easily defendable land, and the borderline in these parts was consequently in dispute much later than elsewhere. This was Armstrong country — probably the toughest and boldest of all the Border families in the fifteenth and early sixteenth centuries.

It would be logical for the border to follow the Esk to the sea, but of course it does not. Following a treaty made in

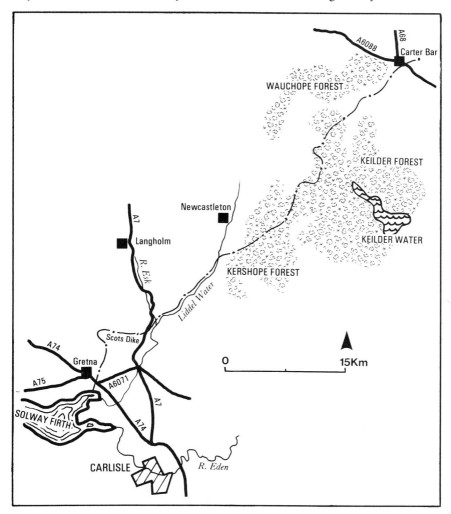

The Blacksmith's shop, Gretna Green

1552, it veers due west for about five miles to join the much smaller River Sark. The line between the two waters was marked by the Scots Dike, an earth and stone wall which can still be made out near the A7, 2 miles south of Canonbie.

The border follows the winding Sark, passing the site of the battle of Solway Moss (1542), to Gretna and the sea. It is the end of a 110-mile journey, a wandering journey indeed when you consider that the straight-line distance from Gretna to Berwick is only 70 miles.

Gretna's main claim to fame is, of course, as the place where many runaway marriages once took place. Up to 1940, it was possible for eloping couples to be married by declaration, and the smithy at Gretna Green was the first

place many of them reached after crossing the border. The marriage trade has ceased now that a residential qualification has been introduced, but many souvenirs and curios are on show at the museum at the smithy. Although the smithy was the most famous place for runaway marriages, and became more popular because of its fame, such betrothals could in fact take place at any house or shop, provided there were witnesses to the declaration.

Crossing the border has always been a significant event, whether for romantic, martial, or peaceful reasons. Now that we have traced it from coast to coast, let us stay on the Scottish side, and begin to work back eastwards, looking at the Border counties in more detail. There is no shortage of things to see!

3 East Dumfriesshire___

This is the part of our area which is administratively outside the Borders Region, but it is very much 'border country' and logically therefore should be included. Many people make their way into Scotland via the M6 and A74 and even if going further into Borders itself, would pass through the area covered by this chapter.

I will cover the area from east to west, starting down by the border and working upwards to a point where it is logical to hand over to the next county to be covered, Peeblesshire. The first 'way in' is therefore the A7 road, which crosses the border at the Scots Dike, already mentioned, and heads more or less due north towards Hawick. As far as Langholm, the first town of any size, it follows the fine valley of the River Esk.

Langholm is, in appearance, a true Border town. It sits in a narrow valley and has among its prominent buildings the mills one expects to find further north, on the Tweed. At one time it was said that the most expensive suiting cloth in the world was produced here. Langholm is divided into a New Town (Meikleholm, built in the 1770s to a regular pattern) and an Old Town, the original burgh under the Dukes of Buccleuch. As three rivers join here, there are several fine bridges. At least one of them had as an apprentice workman Thomas Telford. The man destined to become such a great engineer was born in Westerkirk, in Eskdale.

Also from Westerkirk was one General Sir John Malcolm, a distinguished soldier who became Governor of Bombay and is buried in Westminster Abbey. There is a 100-foot tower to his memory on the summit of Whita Hill above the town; an excellent short walk giving fine views southwards to the border. Sir John had three brothers; they were all knighted, and there is a statue to the one who chose the Navy, and duly became an admiral, beside the Town Hall. Another of Langholm's sons to achieve fame in recent times was the poet C.M. Grieve, better known by his pseudonym Hugh MacDiarmid.

At Langholm we encounter our first Common Riding; this one traditionally takes place on the last Friday in July. As mentioned in the introduction, an odd feature of the day is that the colours worn by the Cornet for his ride are those of the winner of the Epsom Derby each year. This practice has been carried on for 100 years but its origins are not known — perhaps a Langholm man owned a Derby winner in the 1880s?

If you are in Langholm for the Riding, be prepared for an early start. The day's events begin at 5am with a procession led by a flute band, up to Whita Hill, where a hound trail race is held, starting at 6.30am. This is a most exciting spectacle, with the hounds following a scent previously laid, and great competition to find the winner. The Langholm Classic, as it is known, is considered the top event of its kind in the Borders.

At 8.30am the Cornet takes the Town Standard round the old and new towns for the first Fair Crying, when the riding is announced to all and sundry. There follows the gallop up the Kirkwynd to Whitta Yett and Castle Craigs, where the fair is cried again. On returning to

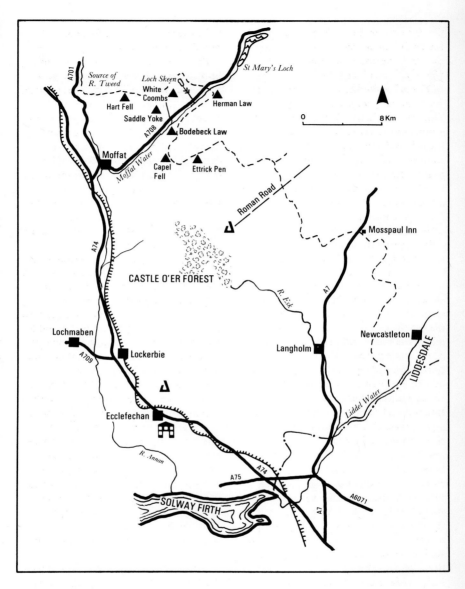

the town the horsemen are met by schoolchildren carrying heather besoms, and everyone goes to the Market Place for another crying. The horsemen then ford the River Ewes to Castleholm, where the race known as Cornet's Chase is run.

There is no let-up in the afternoon — more horse racing, foot races and other sports, wrestling, and highland dancing are all enjoyed and in the evening (for those with energy left!) there is an open air dance, including the Common Riding Polka led by the principals. Finally, the

Cornet returns the Town Standard and the festivities are over. An exhausting day, but one not to be forgotten by visitor and resident alike.

The A7 continues up the valley of the Ewes, passing some charmingly-named places — Unthank, Crude Hill, Castlewink, and Butter Hill among them — to cross into Roxburghshire at the watershed where the Mosspaul Inn stands. If you are heading this way and need a break, there is a fine walk from the Inn up to Wisp Hill, on the west of the road. It is a pretty steep ascent, but nowhere difficult, and from Wisp Hill you can either turn south to Whin Fell or north to Comb Hill before returning to your starting point.

Our next valley is Eskdale, which strikes off north-westwards from Langholm and runs for 20 miles in typical rolling Border hills through country where the sheep and the conifers far outnumber the people. The very large parish of Eskdalemuir and Westerkirk counts less than a thousand souls today, though the number of ruined farms and steadings tell that it was not always thus.

The road (B709) follows the Esk through Westerkirk into Castle O'er Forest. On the B723, which joins it, there is a picnic site provided by the Forestry Commission, and you can walk into the forest for a little way if you wish. Further up the valley is Eskdalemuir, where a weather station has been faithfully recording excesses of various kinds for a good many years. Some of the lowest temperatures suffered each winter usually come from here, and in June 1953 Eskdalemuir was in the news again — not for a heatwave, unfortunately, but because no less than $3\frac{1}{2}$in of rain fell in *one hour* — far more than usually descends in a month! There is a plaque on a bridge nearby marking this feat, the previous bridge having

been swept away by the force of the rapidly rising floodwater.

Returning to the A74, the next town northwards is Ecclefechan. The odd-looking name actually has a very logical root — the church *(eaglais)* of St Fechan, a sixth-century Celtic missionary. In the little town is the Arched House, birthplace of Thomas Carlyle and now, owned by the National Trust for Scotland, holding a collection of his manuscripts and letters. The house is open to visitors from early April to the end of October, every day except Sunday. Carlyle is buried in the kirkyard in Ecclefechan.

A little way north of Ecclefechan, near Middlebie, are two substantial reminders of Roman times. Birrens is a fort which has been extensively excavated. The ditches and ramparts are clearly visible. Burnswark is thought to have been used as a training ground for siege warfare; on a clear day, it has fine views over the Solway estuary.

Six miles to the north of Ecclefechan is the market town of Lockerbie, with a population of just under 3,000. It has a 9-hole golf course and facilities for bowls and tennis. The cattle market is one of the most important in the area. Lamb Hill, above the town, is named from the Lockerbie Lamb Sales, which began here in the seventeenth century. So profitable were these sales that the town was able to buy Lamb Hill as public ground — and have £10,000 over to build the fine town hall.

Glaswegians will find an echo of their city 3 miles south-east of Lockerbie at Castlemilk, the seat of the Jardine family. The present house dates from 1866. If you travel north-west for the same distance from the town you will find another Jardine stronghold at Spedlins. This fifteenth-century pele tower has a prison cell within the thick-

Carlyle's Birthplace, Ecclefechan

ness of one of the walls — a horrid place to be incarcerated.

From Lockerbie, the A74 passes through pleasant country in the valley of the River Annan for a further 15 miles to reach the turn-off for Moffat — to me, a true Border town, despite its position at the very edge of our region. Mineral springs were discovered here in the mid-eighteenth century, and Moffat became a fashionable place to visit. It still has a slightly genteel air with several fine town houses with large gardens. In the centre of the town is the handsome square; and

in the centre of the square is the Colvin Fountain, surmounted by its famous ram. It proclaims clearly that this is sheep country.

The town park offers bowls and tennis, and there is an 18-hole golf course on the outskirts, but for me Moffat is a centre for walking. To the north and east are splendid hills, and two longish excursions will give the flavour of the area very well.

The first walk leaves the town due north, following the valley of the Birnock Water by Archbank. Walk up

Moffat

this valley for about four miles, with the bulk of Swatte Fell looming ever nearer. It is a straightforward ascent by the left-hand of the two streams at the head of the valley. Once on the ridge, follow it round the head of the valley which contains Auchencat Burn and so gain Hart Fell. The summit has a triangulation pillar and stone shelter.

From Hart Fell, head first north then east, keeping to the high ground over Hartfell Rig and then southwards onto Priest Craig and Saddle Yoke. Look down to your right into the deep gash of the Blackshope Valley and feel for the runners who have to make that descent — and then climb the equally steep slope opposite — during the annual Moffat Hill Race, run in early October. I took part once, so I know how tough that scrambling drop and hard climb is on the legs and lungs!

To end the walk, you can either take the hill runners' route, though more slowly, and then use the track alongside Blackshope Burn to the main road; or continue along the ridge from Saddle Yoke, descending a little less steeply. Either way, you will reach the A708 at or near Capplegill. Unless you have transport waiting here, the walk is best done (in summer) on a Thursday, when the Harrier bus service passes this way going to Moffat (timetables from the regional tourist board or enquire locally). The walk is about twelve miles with a fair amount of climbing, and as in poor visibility the navigation could be tricky, keep it for a good day.

The second walk also demands a good day. This one starts from Capplegill (buses from Moffat) and crosses the Moffat Water, through Bodesbeck, to follow the track that leads over the Potburn Pass into the Ettrick Valley. We do not, however, go down with the track, but at the pass turn left and climb smartly up for 600ft on to Bodesbeck Law.

Grey Mares' Tail

From here it is a genuine highway, keeping to the ridge (also the regional boundary) over Bell Craig, Mirk Side, and Andrewhinney Hill to Herman Law — a superb ridge walk of 6 miles. From Andrewhinney there are stunning views across the valley northwards to Loch Skeen and the Grey Mare's Tail water-fall. From Herman Law head north-eastwards round the side of East Muchra Hill, into the valley of the Whithope Burn, to pick up the track curving round to Tibbie Shiels Inn by St Mary's Loch — a splendid place to end a walk, especially if the inn is open! If it is not, there is a teabar nearby in the summer months. This glorious walk is also about twelve miles, but could take up a full day with no difficulty at all — so splendid is the country and so wide are the views.

Having seen the Grey Mare's Tail from above, let us now look at it from below, taking the A708 Selkirk road from Moffat to the car park at the foot of the Tail Burn. The fall and the surrounding hills are in the care of the National Trust for Scotland, having been purchased in 1962. Loch Skeen sits in a perfect example of a hanging valley or high corrie, scooped out by the forces of ice during the last Ice Age some 12,000-15,000 years ago.

From the car park by the roadside, a path is signposted up the east side of the fall to the loch. Please follow the marked route — this is a very steep hillside and there have been some nasty accidents here. The path has had a lot of work done on it in recent years and the most eroded parts are now bypassed or have steps. Take your time going up to the loch — it is very steep! — and enjoy the widening views across the valley. You might like to extend the walk westwards from Loch Skeen up on to the summit of White Coomb, a grassy plateau at nearly

2,700 feet. You can either return the way you came or go down the ridge south-westwards to Carrifran, for a walk of about five miles in matchless surroundings.

One more notable landscape feature demands our attention before we pass into Peeblesshire. Take the A701 road north out of Moffat and climb up to the watershed at over 1,300 feet. Just over the rise is the source of the Tweed; on this side the eye is irresistibly drawn to the great scoop known as the Devil's Beef Tub. This, too, was formed by glacial action, and is hardly less dramatic than Loch Skeen. Scott, in *Redgauntlet,* had the Laird of Summer-trees making his escape by rolling down the Tub from top to bottom — not a thing that I would recommend anyone to try!

By the roadside is a stone commemorating John Hunter, a Covenanter shot here by Douglas's Dragoons in 1685. With this rather grim reminder of a troubled past, we leave Dumfriesshire and re-enter Borders Region, into Peeblesshire by the side of the infant Tweed.

4 Peeblesshire

Leaving the Devil and his Beef Tub behind, the traveller on the A701 crosses the watershed and enters Peeblesshire. Within a couple of miles, the shallow basin on the right (east) of the road gives up the source of the Tweed, third longest river in Scotland at 90 miles. By the side of the road is a small memorial to a sad event — the death of a mail carrier in a fearsome blizzard many years ago.

The road runs down through a great deal of young forest and the infant Tweed is soon joined by enough side burns to give it shape and power. Not surprisingly, some of this water-power has been harnessed and at the small village of Tweedsmuir, a side-road leads up to three reservoirs — Talla, Fruin, and the recently completed Megget. Whatever one thinks of altering the

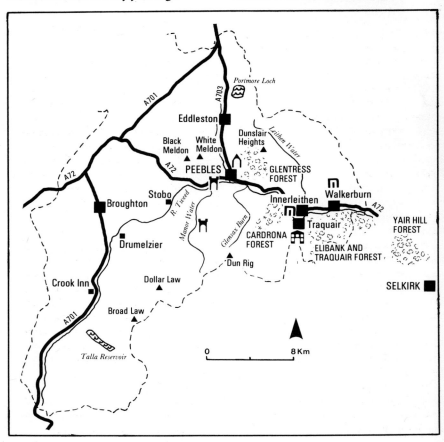

countryside in this way, it makes a wonderfully scenic drive, and at the high point of the road is the Megget Stone, an ancient boundary marker.

Megget Stone is an alternative start to Tweedsmuir for the walk to Broad Law, at 840m the highest point in the Borders. It is a straightforward walk over easy ground, mostly well-cropped grass and broad ridges. The walk goes over Cairn Law and the oddly-named Porridge Cairn, and the return can be made in any one of three ways — either back to your starting point if you are self-driven, or, if you have an obliging driver, by extending it and making it a rather more satisfying outing.

There is a radio station at the summit of Broad Law, and a surfaced track leads all the way up to it from Tweedsmuir. You can use this for your descent route, or you can make a very pleasant loop by continuing north-eastwards from Broad Law over Cramalt Craig and Dun Law, dropping down to the path that leads from the Manor Valley to St Mary's Loch and walking down to the Tibbie Shiels Inn on the lochside.

If you decide to go down to Tweedsmuir, your companion could wait for you at the Crook Inn, just north of the village. This is one of the oldest Border inns, and has been a meeting-place for travellers since 1604. In the seventeenth century the inn was the scene of many a secret Covenanters' meeting and later gave inspiration to Robert Burns for his poem *Willie Wastle's Wife,* written in the old kitchen, which is now the bar. John Buchan, born nearby, used the area as background for several of his books, and took the title of Lord Tweedsmuir when he was ennobled in later life.

More recently, the inn saw a piece of Scottish mountaineering history enacted; it was the chosen location for the first-ever meet of the Scottish

Mountaineering Club in 1891. Members braved the ascent of Broad Law — a humble beginning for a club which has achieved so much in the ensuing decades.

Ten miles or so north of Tweedsmuir, a right turn leads to the village of Drumelzier, one of the many reputed resting places of the magician Merlin. It was also the scene of a prediction come true, in 1603. The prediction was one of many made during his long life (1225-1307) by Thomas the Rhymer, actually Thomas Learmounth of Earlston. He said:

When Tweed and Powsail meet at Merlin's grave,
Scotland and England shall one monarch have.

On the day when James VI of Scotland was crowned in London as James I of England, it is reported that the Tweed rose to an extraordinary level and ran into the Powsail Burn. It has never happened since. On a rocky knoll just north of the village is another reminder of history — the ruins of Tinnis Castle, blown up during one of the frequent Border feuds between families — in this case the Tweedies and Flemings.

A little further along the road is a more tranquil scene — the arboretum at Dawyck. The gardens were first developed by the Naesmyth family, who lived at Dawyck until 1897, when it was acquired by Colonel F.R.S. Balfour. He carried out a great deal of planting, planning and development, work which was continued by his son, Lt-Col A.N. Balfour. Lt-Col Balfour handed the gardens into the care of the Royal Botanic Society of Edinburgh in 1979.

There are several rare specimens of trees, including Dawyck Beeches and the weeping spruce, brought here from

Oregon in 1908. The original Dawyck Beech can be seen through the yew arch about 250 metres south-east of the house. There are several magnificent Douglas Firs, the largest specimen measuring over fifty metres in height. It is believed that the great Swedish botanist Linnaeus visited Dawyck, and planted one of the first larches in Scotland, in 1725.

There is a long-established heronry in the Lour Wood, and many other birds including woodpeckers, kingfishers, crossbills, tree creepers, and dippers can be seen at different times of the year. The arboretum is open to the public, and there is a car park signposted from the B712. Dawyck House, rebuilt in 1830 following a fire which largely destroyed the original house, is not open but the

Talla Reservoir

Castle on the right, superbly set on a bluff high above the river. The castle is an outstanding example of a Borders pele-tower and is well worth a visit. It is open from Easter to mid-October.

The castle, an L-shaped tower, is believed to have been built in the early fourteenth century and remodelled several times, lastly in the eighteenth century. It served as a home, and seat of power for the Fraser and Hay families, as well as a fortress.

The estate passed by inheritance in 1810 to the Earls of Wemyss (now also Earls of March) and since 1952 has been in the care of the Wemyss and March Estates. The present Earl, who at the time of writing is also President of the National Trust for Scotland, has directed much of the recent work of restoration.

So to the Royal Burgh of Peebles — a comely town indeed. Peebles received its royal charter from David II in 1367, but it was settled long before that, and there was a stronghold here in the twelfth century — natural enough, given the town's position at the confluence of five valleys and with a ford across the Tweed.

Peebles today has a population of about 6,000, and no shortage of facilities for the visitor. An excellent golf course, swimming, riding, fishing, tennis, and a trim track, all are available. There are two good camp and caravan sites, and a wide variety of hotel and guest house accommodation, from the famous Hydro — the largest hotel in the Borders — down to bed and breakfast places taking only two or three people. The Tourist Information Centre, just off the High Street and clearly signposted, is open from Easter to mid-October.

Many of Peebles' more interesting buildings are associated with famous

gardens can be visited, and are at their best in the summer months.

The B712 road continues past Stobo Castle, now a very expensive health clinic, and, running beside the Tweed all the way, joins A72 for the final 4 miles through beautiful woods and into the county town, Peebles. Just before reaching the town you cannot fail to notice the dramatic outline of Neidpath

Peebles

sons of the town, and a Town Trail was laid out as a contribution to European Architectural Heritage Year. A leaflet is available from the TIC or local shops. A good place to start is Chambers Institution, near the TIC. The building dates from the sixteenth century but was extensively modernised in the nineteenth century, by which time it was in the hands of the Chambers family, founders of the Edinburgh publishing company famous for their dictionaries and encyclopaedias. William Chambers gave the building to the burgh of Peebles and it has been used as a civic centre, meeting place and museum ever since.

Walking west along the attractive High Street, you pass the County and Tontine Hotels, both buildings of character and history. The County's eighteenth-century facade conceals a much older interior with a vaulted room, thick walled for security. The Tontine (the name derives from the method of investment used to fund the property)

dates from 1808 and has an elegant dining room with a music gallery.

A little further along on the left is the entrance to Parliament Square — so called after an emergency session held here in 1346. The steps leading down from the Square are called the Stinking Stair, probably from the smell arising from a tannery once sited at the bottom.

Across the street is Bank House, once the home of John Buchan and still housing the firm of writers (solicitors) which bears his name. The street has as its handsome endpiece Peebles Old Parish Church, built on the site of the medieval Peebles Castle and the centre-piece of some of the Beltane Festival ceremonies described below. For now, a right turn across the burn known as The Cuddy, a walk along Biggiesknowe (a name corrupted from Bridge House Knowe) and a left turn will lead you to the thirteenth-century Cross Kirk with its atmosphere of serenity, despite the busy town around it.

PLACES TO VISIT AROUND PEEBLES

Chambers Institution, Peebles
Civic centre and museum.

Cross Kirk, Peebles
Thirteenth-century church, now a ruin.

Dawyck Arboretum
Many fine trees, woodland walks, heronry, gardens.

Neidpath Castle
Excellent example of border pele-tower, overlooking River Tweed.

Cademuir
Celtic fort outside Peebles with excellent views.

Kailzie
Wild gardens, duck pond, pheasantry, plant centre, pottery, art gallery.

Traquair House
Oldest continually-occupied house in Scotland. Fine rooms, brewhouse, craft workers, gardens, maze.

Innerleithen, Traquair and Glen Museum, Innerleithen
History and traditions of the area on display.

Scottish Museum of Wool Textiles, Walkerburn
Displays progress of the wool industry, produce shop, machinery.

The church was built by order of King Alexander III after the discovery of a magnificent cross on the site, and rumour has it that St Nicholas is buried here. The kirk is now a listed monument and is open to view.

In the third week of June — midsummer — Peebles comes alive for the Beltane Festival, inaugurated in 1897 to mark the Diamond Jubilee of Queen Victoria but really a revival of a very much older tradition. There is no shortage of ceremony; the week begins with the inauguration of the Warden of Cross Kirk and a united church service. Wednesday evening sees the installation of the Cornet, a young man of the town, and the bussing of the Burgh flag by the Cornet's Lass. Cornet, Lass and Supporters then ride the Marches, halting at Neidpath Castle for another ceremony

of installation — Warden of Neidpath, usually a prominent local figure. Recent Wardens have included David Steel MP, the Liberal Party leader, whose large constituency includes Peebles, and Lt-Col Aidan Sprot of Haystoun, a large estate just south of the town.

On Thursday evening the Cornet's Walk takes him round the town, presumably for approval by the populace, and he and the Beltane Queen (a young lady of grace and charm from the primary school final year) are escorted to their homes after a Grand Beltane Concert. Friday evening sees a fancy dress parade, and on Saturday a superbly enjoyable day starts with the Ride Out and Proclamation of the Beltane Fair, followed by the crowning of the Beltane Queen on the steps of the parish church. Over 400 children take

Neidpath Castle, Peebles

part in the pageantry and afterwards a long and gloriously colourful procession of floats winds its way slowly round the town, led and interspersed with bands of all kinds.

In the afternoon there are sports and Highland Dancing competitions in Hay Lodge Park and in the evening the moving spectacle of a full pipe band beating retreat in the High Street. Given the right weather, it is a wonderful day.

Peebles is an ideal centre for walking or fishing holidays. Details of the latter can be obtained from local tackle shops or the addresses given in the Further Information, and there are beats enough to satisfy the most energetic angler. The walking can be sampled either along or around Glensax, a very beautiful valley south of the town. The more straightforward walk goes out through Gallowhill and turns right, through the Haystoun estate and on to the track in Glensax. Follow the track for about three miles to Glensax Lodge, which has lost some of its former splendour but is still used by shooting parties. Return to Peebles the same way — even though you are retracing your steps you will not be bored with such splendid hill scenery around.

If you want to sample those hills, a strenuous but by no means difficult circuit starts the same way. Instead of turning right through Haystoun, go straight on through the pretty Gipsy Glen and up on to the old droving road that climbs the ridge east of Glensax. At the start of the climb the walls either side of the track show how wide it was when it was regularly used by cattle on their way to the markets of England.

Follow the ridge over Kailzie Hill and Birkscairn Hill, with superb views over Tweeddale, and keep to the high ground, following old fence posts, all the way up to Dun Rig, whose survey pillar is, at 742m, the high point of the walk. It gives a fine panorama of the Border hills, from the Eildons to Broad Law. Work round the head of the Glensax Burn and on to Hundleshope Heights. Keep to the right hand ridge on the descent and you will find yourself dropping down into Glensax to pick up the clear track along the glen, through Haystoun, and so back to the town. This is a circuit of about twelve miles, and makes a most invigor-

From Dun Rig to the east side of Glensax

ating spring or autumn walk.

A shorter walk with much to commend it starts at Tweed Bridge. Walk west along the river and turn up the hill at the waymark, a little way before the wood. Turn right up a road and follow it when it becomes a track, turning first left then right to a stile. Follow the path round the edge of South Park Wood — a very interesting place for birdlife. On rejoining the road, walk downhill and turn right over Old Manor Bridge, built in 1703. The return path follows the river bank all the way, passing under a splendid railway bridge (now disused) and below the frowning bluff on which Neidpath Castle stands. The walk is about $4\frac{1}{2}$ miles and makes a very pleasant outing for a summer evening.

From the Manor Bridge, a minor road leads south for 9 miles into the beautiful Manor Valley. It is a splendidly scenic drive, passing another tower at Castlehill and a fort at Glenrath romantically named Macbeth's Castle. From the road end there are numerous walking possibilities; an outline of two will give the flavour.

West of the valley, the ascent of Dollar Law is steep but without difficulty, following the edge of a forestry plantation up the ridge to the survey pillar, at 818m second only in height in the Borders to Broad Law. To the east, a clear track leads through the hills (really more south than east), under Bitch Craig and in 6 miles (10km) down to Glengaber on the back road that follows the Megget Water down to St Mary's Loch. There is an inn at the end of this walk; so it could be done both ways in a day with a pleasant break in between.

Another, shorter walk well worth doing from Peebles takes the road through Kingsmuir to its end at Tantah. Past the farm and through a gate, a clear path winds up on to Cademuir, site of a Celtic fort. It is an easy walk but the rewards are great in terms of the view. The Tweed winds far below; across it to north and east are the Moorfoot Hills, while to the south and west the hills of Manor and Megget stand out. In autumn, with the heather at its best, it makes a glorious scene.

The back road from Peebles to Innerleithen (B7062) yields two treasures to the visitor. First, 3 miles from Peebles, is Kailzie (pronounced Kailey). The name derives from an old word Kelioch or Kaillow, meaning a wooded glen, and first appears in records in 1296. After being in the hands of the Tweedie family for several centuries, the property passed through a number of owners before the present owner, Mrs Richard, took it over in 1962. At that time the old house was demolished and Mrs Richard conceived the idea of developing and improving the gardens. They now provide a wide variety of habitats.

The Wild Garden is at its best in the spring, when daffodils and bluebells provide a magnificent carpet of colour. The trees include an ancient copper beech and a larch which rivals that at Dawyck for age — it was apparently brought to Mr Plenderleith of Kailzie from Dawyck in 1725. Azaleas and rhododendrons give a fine show in May and June.

The 'Major's Walk' is rich in plants including primulas, polyanthus, and more azaleas and rhododendrons. A cupressus walk leads to the duck pond, from where there are fine views across the Tweed. There are over twenty varieties of duck in the pond. Not far away is the Pheasantry, with a dozen varieties of these colourful game birds; two recent arrivals are Iranian eagle owls.

The plant centre has many interesting plants and shrubs for sale as well as

Traquair House

preserves made on the estate. Part of the old stable block has been carefully converted into an attractive tearoom, an interesting note being that the doors were brought here from St Andrew's church in Peebles when it was demolished in 1980. Next door to the tearoom is a small art gallery featuring the work of local artists.

Kailzie is open every day from March to October; as well as the attractions of the gardens and woods, there are holiday cottages to let throughout the year.

Four miles further east is the entrance to Traquair, the oldest continually inhabited house in Scotland — its first charter was granted by Alexander I in 1107. The house has changed little in appearance since the seventeenth century, but you will not use the original

Mary Queen of Scots relics in Traquair House

entrance through the Bear Gates. They were locked after Prince Charlie passed through here in 1745, and tradition has it that they will not be reopened until the Stuarts are restored to the throne of Britain. The house contains a number of relics relating to the Stuarts, including the cradle of James VI, and many other treasures and works of art.

Traquair is, however, very much a living house. The present laird, Mr Peter Maxwell Stuart, brews Traquair Ale in the eighteenth-century brewhouse, sited (significantly?) below the chapel, and powerful stuff it is, too; definitely to be savoured in small quantities and not quaffed by the pint! Traquair is a centre for craft workers with a number of outbuildings having been converted for use by potters, weavers, woodworkers and others.

There are woodland and riverside walks laid out and the tearoom, in a 1745 cottage in the walled garden, provides refreshments. Traquair is open from Easter to October and deserves at least half a day to itself. Your stay may be inadvertently extended if you take in the maze!

Between Kailzie and Traquair, Cardrona Forest offers a picnic area and a choice of three forestry walks, all of them clearly signposted. On the east side of the forest are the rather overgrown ruins of a pele tower.

Traquair village is the start of one of the Borders' best-known walks, the drove road over Minch Moor to Selkirk. The route climbs up through mature forest to pass the 'Cheese Well', where an offering of cheese is said to placate the fairies and thus safeguard the traveller. The route winds on over Brown Knowe and Broomy Law to the distinctive triple cairn of the Three Brethren. From here there are three choices of route. Straight on leads down Long Philip Burn to the outskirts of Selkirk (if you can pass Philipburn House, a hotel noted for its fine cuisine). A left turn takes you down through Yair Forest to the A707 at Yair, and a right turn leads to Broadmeadows. This was the route taken by walkers in May 1931 preceding the opening of Scotland's first youth hostel, at Broadmeadows, a walk repeated in May 1981 to mark the SYHA's Golden Jubilee.

From Traquair it is a short mile along the road to the mill town of Innerleithen, whose patron saint, St Ronan, has a well dedicated to him on the hill north of the town. He is commemorated each year in the Cleikum Ceremony, and the emblems used in that ceremony, along with many other items relating to the history and traditions of the area, can be seen in the Innerleithen, Traquair and Glen Museum, housed in the former Burgh Council offices and open on Wednesdays and Saturdays between April and October.

Two miles east of Innerleithen is the smaller town of Walkerburn, where no visitor should fail to stop at the Scottish Museum of Woollen Textiles in the Tweedvale Mill complex. The progress of the industry is recreated from the early days of hand spinning and weaving up to factory production and modern high speed machinery. There are evocative early photographs and a fascinating display of plants and flowers which were traditionally used to produce dyes. Produce can be bought at the mill shop and refreshments are available. The museum is open daily from Easter to the end of October.

The Tweed Valley Hotel, at the east end of the town, is a notable base for sporting holidays. The angler, walker, and hunter are all well catered for, and the cuisine is more than sufficient both in quality and quantity for the needs of the hungriest holidaymaker.

As this is almost the eastern boundary of Peeblesshire, let us make our way back a little to Innerleithen and the start of one of my favourite walks in the Borders. It's a longish 15 miles and will occupy a full day, but it can easily be shortened if you want a shorter outing. The walk starts by turning north along the little road directly opposite the B709. Turn left over a stile in the woods, and on reaching the radio mast at St Ronan's

Innerleithen, Tweed valley

Well, turn right for the sharp pull up to Lee Pen. It's a climb which will tax anyone, but the views are opening up all the time, giving plenty of good reasons for stopping.

Lee Pen, at 502m, is not the peak it appears to be as you climb, but the abrupt end of a long ridge leading northwest over Black Knowe, Black Law (trig pillar, 538m) and on to the high TV booster mast at Dunslair Heights (602m). If you go no further, you will have enjoyed a splendid walk, with wide views south over the Tweed Valley and north across the Moorfoot Hills. There is a fair amount of forestry development taking place in these hills, but the ridge itself is clear.

Dunslair Heights is the top of Glentress Forest (oddly named — the small settlement of Glentress is miles away in the valley of the Leithen Water) and it is a simple matter to cut short the walk here by dropping down through the forest, either to the car park at Horsbrugh or to Peebles. There are several forest walks in Glentress, starting from the forestry office at Horsbrugh, which

is on the A72 about two miles east of Peebles. There is also a forest wayfaring course — a non-competitive version of orienteering. Glentress is one of the more mature of the Borders forests and, as well as being very pleasant to walk through, has been used for a number of orienteering championship events.

I hope, however, that you will wish to carry on along the ridge from Dunslair, as I believe the best of the walk is in its second part. It follows the forestry fence over the sharp knob of Makeness Kipps and the undulations of Cardon Law and Hog Knowes on to the broad back of Dundreich, a very fine hill and, at 623m, the high point of the walk in every way. From here, on a clear day, there is a marvellous view northwards taking in the whole of Edinburgh, the Pentland Hills, and the Firth of Forth. Gladhouse Reservoir, a major wintering-ground for waterbirds, is visible a little east of north.

Descend westwards from Dundreich to hit the track running south from Portmore Loch (which is private ground) and follow it through the farmstead at

Boreland to the main road just north of Eddleston. At the time of writing there was a very good teashop here, but its opening hours are somewhat limited — check locally before you take its refreshing presence for granted! There are hourly buses from Eddleston back to Peebles or Innerleithen.

Looking east from Dundreich across the valley of the South Esk (a much shorter river than the one of the same name in Angus) the eye is drawn to Blackhope Scar, at 652m the highest point in Lothian Region. (Only just — the summit is right on the boundary.) To the east again is the northward continuation of the B709 from Innerleithen to Heriot, a drive well worth taking for its scenic quality. There are also any number of possible walks either side of the valley.

Leaving Innerleithen and passing one of a number of fairly remarkable small golf courses in the Borders, there is a good view across the town to the point known as St Ronan's Well. The name was actually popularised by Sir Walter Scott, who published a novel of that name in 1824. It led to Innerleithen having a long period of popularity as a spa, visited for its mineral waters. St Ronan's Games are still held here each year, in July. On the final day there is a firework display on Caerlee Hill and a modern 'saint' throws an effigy of the Devil onto a bonfire — the Cleikum ceremony.

You may also notice that one of the streets on your left as you drive out of town is called Strand. A walk around Innerleithen would also reveal a Bond Street, Morningside, and a Piccadilly — idiosyncrasies of the last Earl of Traquair. Of note, too, is Caerlee Mill behind Chapel Street. It was established in 1790 by Alexander Brodie in order to give employment to the young of the area and to make use of the plentiful supply of excellent wool available locally. Other factories and mills followed, and Innerleithen is still renowned as a centre for knitwear and woollen yarn.

The road climbs steadily with fine hills to either side following the Leithen Water as far as Dod Hill, where it turns right to run alongside the equally attractive Glentress Water. From the steading of Glentress a splendid walk leads up to the ridge of Windlestraw Law, with the oddly-named Deaf Heights available as an extension for the energetic. Across the valley to the west, Whitehope Law is a sharper pull but is worth the effort for its views.

The road climbs to 364m at the watershed — a useful starting-point for the ascent of Blackhope Scar, if you wish to take that hill on its own. It is a fairly tough climb over rough ground, and a slightly easier alternative is to go round to the steading at Blackhope and follow the Blackhope Water up, diverting either side of it in due course to gain the ridges leading to the Scar.

On the downhill run, the road keeps by Dewar Burn until that watercourse becomes Heriot Water — a lonely run past a number of isolated houses and farms, before meeting the A7 at the village of Heriot. The temptation here is to turn left towards Edinburgh, but it is one that I at least must reject. I must return south, across the Tweed to leave Peeblesshire and enter the old county of Selkirkshire.

5 Selkirkshire

Geographically, Selkirkshire is a most odd shape, with its boundaries taking many a twist and turn, reflecting the turns of history and fortune which have divided and joined the communities and estates it contains, over hundreds of years. It is a county rich in scenery, historic houses, monastic ruins, and with plenty of opportunities for the visitor, be he of an enquiring mind or seeking energetic recreation.

Staying with the A72 which brought you from Peebles, you pass through the neat village of Clovenfords, with a fine statue of Sir Walter Scott outside the hotel, to reach Galashiels on Gala Water. With a population of just over 12,000, 'Gala' as it is always known is second only to Hawick in size among the Border towns, and would no doubt see itself as being superior in every other respect. It certainly warrants a long stay.

Gala hosts one of the famous seven-a-side Rugby tournaments in April each year, and its festival, the Braw Lads Gathering, is held in late June or early

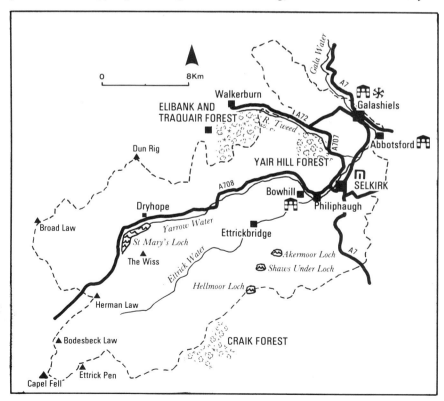

Galashiels

July. It has a most unusual motto —
'Soor Plums' — arising from an incident
in 1337 when, after one of the many
skirmishes of the time, a party of English
soldiers gathered on the meadows at
Netherdale and paused to eat some of
the fine wild plums growing there. They
were surprised by local militia, who
killed them and put their bodies in a
trench still known as Englishmen's Syke.

Galashiels has been a weaving town
for at least 700 years, but its modern
growth can be traced back to 1790, when
George Mercer built here the first real
factory in Scotland. It does not survive,
but Valley Mill, behind Market Street,
does and is a fine example of nineteenth-
century mill architecture. This was the

home of Scottish Tweed — not, as many think, named after the river, but from a slip of the pen when a clerk transcribed the word twill (pronounced 'tweel') and put a 'd' at the end.

The Scottish College of Textiles was established in Gala in 1909 and still thrives. There are several mill shops, selling tartans, tweeds, wools and other knitted materials. Addresses are given in the Further Information and opening times can be ascertained locally. Of equal interest is the Tweedbank Craft Centre across the water, where a number of craft workers operate and can be seen.

Galashiels has a 9-hole golf course at Torwoodlee and a full 18-hole course at Ladhope. Both are open to visitors.

Evening in Galashiels

Fishing is available on both Tweed and Gala waters; details, and any gear you might need, are available from the long-established tackle and sports shop of J. & A. Turnbull in Bank Street. Permits for single or multiple days' fishing can be obtained here. Pony trekking is available at the Galashiels Riding Centre at Netherbarns, on the Selkirk road. Horses can be supplied for day treks or longer periods, and advice on where to ride. Horses can also be hired for the Braw Lads Gathering.

The Gathering was established in 1930, and takes its name from a well-known poem by Robert Burns (also a fine song). The events associated with the Gathering stretch over a week, but the principal happenings start on the Wednesday evening with a rideout to Torwoodlee to cut a sod of turf and take a stone from the tower; on this evening there is also a fancy dress parade. On the Friday the two principals, the Braw Lad and Braw Lass, are invested, and Saturday's ceremonies begin with the Braw Lad receiving the Burgh flag.

The party proceeds to the Raid Stane (site of the skirmish which led to the 'soor plums' episode); the three lads are adorned with a spray of leaves from a plum tree, and the party then fords the Tweed to Abbotsford to be received by the Scott family. After returning to the town, the rideout ends with an act of homage at the war memorial. In the afternoon there are children's sports and other events at Netherdale.

At the war memorial is the statue of the Reiver, a famous landmark. Here too is the clock tower, where the bells play the old air 'Gala Water' every evening at eight o'clock. This is the air to which Burns wrote the poem 'Braw, Braw Lads', in 1793. Burns has a statue at the foot of Lawyer's Brae, and there is

Old Gala House, Galashiels

inevitably one of Sir Walter Scott, in St John Street.

Scott is however principally associated with the lovely house of Abbotsford, where he lived from 1811 to his death in 1832. The house is much grander now than it was when Scott bought it — and so is its name, for it was previously known as Cartley or Clarty Hole, meaning 'a dirty place'! The house

is a lasting monument to the man. It is open from March to the end of October, and contains many treasures Scott collected in his lifetime, including Rob Roy's gun, the keys from the Old Tolbooth (gaol) in Edinburgh, and some fine antique furniture. The library is very fine and among its many rare and magnificent books is the first volume ever to be printed in Australia — a unique work indeed.

At Abbotsford, Scott wrote many of his most famous and best-loved works, including *Rob Roy, Heart of Midlothian,* and *Old Mortality* — all part of the series that became known as the Waverley Novels. The house cost him dear, for his grandiose schemes for improvements, tree planting, landscaping, and interior decoration, were all expensive, and he had to write at a forced pace to keep bankruptcy from the door. It undoubtedly had an effect on his health and hastened his end.

Abbotsford is hard against the Roxburghshire border; so we must turn south, down the A7 for the short journey beside Ettrick Water to the ancient burgh of Selkirk. It has been truly said that history has marked the town with an indelible stamp. Its Abbey was founded in 1113 by the man who later became David I; it was already a famous hunting-area for the nobility. William Wallace was proclaimed Guardian of Scotland here, and the town will be forever linked with the sad chapter of Flodden Field.

Sir Walter Scott was Sheriff of Selkirk for thirty-three years, and his statue is prominent in the Market Place. Behind it is the Courtroom, completed in 1803, and at certain times (enquire locally) you can see his bench, chair, and robing-room. There are also copies of the burgh's ancient charters, and letters from Robert Burns, James Hogg, and other notables. A portrait of Scott hangs above the bench. The curfew bell rings from the tower at 8pm each night.

Abbotsford House, Roxburghshire

49

PLACES TO VISIT AROUND GALASHIELS

Valley Mill, Galashiels
Fine example of nineteenth-century mill architecture.

Tweedbank Craft Centre
Potters, weavers, and other artists.

Abbotsford
Home of Sir Walter Scott. Fine rooms, library, mementoes of Scott, gardens.

On the west side of the Market Place is the fascinating Museum of Old Iron-mongery (in Halliwell's Close) with a wonderful collection of household utensils from times past, in a beautifully restored eighteenth-century town house. Nearby, next to the post office, is Robert Douglas's bakery, where the baker made the original Selkirk bannock, a fruit loaf much favoured by Queen Victoria (and thousands of other visitors to the town since!). Douglas used only the finest ingredients — if the best was not available, he did not bake.

Kirk Wynd contains the ruin of the old parish church, and from here there is a lovely view over the Ettrick Water to the hills beyond. The road bridge at the south end of the town was washed away in a flash flood in 1978 and had to be rebuilt. Off Kirk Wynd is Back Row, the oldest part of the town but now with a modern housing development which won a Civic Trust Award in 1971. Local materials were used and the character of the old town has been carefully preserved.

The Public Library, in Chapel Street, contains another excellent museum, this time featuring local history. The building was originally the town jail. It was acquired in 1883 by Thomas Craig-Brown, a former Provost of Selkirk and a noted historian. He had the building refurbished and gave it to the town as a free library. Among the exhibits in the museum is the banner captured from the English at Flodden by one Fletcher, the only Selkirk man to return from the battle alive. According to the story, when he reached the Market Place he could find no words to tell the crowd of the battle. He merely cast the banner on the cobbles in anguish and despair.

The casting is a central feature of Selkirk Common Riding, held in June each year. It starts on a Thursday evening with the Burgh Officer 'crying the Burley' round the town to summon riders to attend next morning. All the trades and professions are represented in the procession which follows, each with its own standard bearer.

On Friday morning there is no lying a-bed; events start at 6am when crowds assemble and follow a band along the High Street, up Back Row and down Kirk Wynd to the tunes *Hail Smiling Morn* and *Lead, Kindly Light*. This *should* guarantee a sunny day! The crowd then goes down to the Ettrick Water to see the Standard Bearer (who must be unmarried and a Selkirk lad) and his party of riders away into the country.

It's a stiff ride they have, too — right up to the Three Brethrens Cairn above Yair Forest and then back by Shawburn Toll, a circuit of about four hours. On their return they gallop up to Market Place for the final, solemn ceremonies. To the old tune *Up wi' the Souters* (souters were shoemakers) the standard Bearer casts his flag, keeping time with the music. Other flags are then cast, the last being the standard borne by the Royal British Legion, in memory of all

PLACES TO VISIT AROUND SELKIRK

Courtroom, Selkirk
Sir Walter Scott's bench, chair, and robing-room.

Museum of Old Ironmongery, Selkirk
Household utensils from two centuries ago.

Selkirk Library
Local history museum, banner from Flodden.

Bowhill
Seat of the Dukes of Buccleuch. Paintings include one by Leonardo. Collection of clocks. Gardens, nature trails, adventure playground.

Blackhouse Tower
Seat of the Douglas family for many centuries.

Souters who have fallen in battle. A short silence is observed and then the pipes play the *Lilting,* the lament for the fallen at Flodden. The Standard Bearer returns the standard to the Provost, and the ceremonies are over.

Flodden is not the only battle commemorated in Selkirk. Just across the river from the town is Philiphaugh, where the royalist forces led byMontrose were defeated in a bloody encounter by Lesley's Covenanting Army in 1645. A hundred years later, Prince Charlie passed this way, stopping in Selkirk for the souters to fit his men with good shoes for their ill-fated march south into England.

There is a fine walk from here, up Long Philip Burn to the Three Brethren. It's a steady climb, but the path is clear

all the way. You can either return by the same route, or turn left at the cairn for Broadmeadows. The youth hostel here was the first to be opened in Scotland, in May 1931, and still offers simple accommodation to the traveller, young or old.

Across the A708 from Broadmeadows is Bowhill, seat of the Duke of Buccleuch. House and grounds are open at Easter and then from May to the end of September. The house dates mainly from the early nineteenth century and contains many magnificent works of art, including the *Madonna and the Yarnwinder,* the only painting by Leonardo da Vinci still in private hands in this country. There are many fine examples of seventeenth- and eighteenth-century furniture and clocks, including a remarkable longcase clock made in 1780 in Fife. It plays eight different Scottish airs, but the mechanism is arranged so that the clock observes the Sabbath — from midnight Saturday to midnight Sunday it is silent!

The grounds are a perfect demonstration of the fact that farming, forestry, conservation, amenity and sport can all be reconciled. There are fine gardens, nature trails and woodland walks, an adventure playground for youngsters, and all the while the running of the estate goes on. Bowhill is well equipped for visitors, with ample car and coach parking (free), access for wheelchairs, gift shop and tea rooms. It should not be missed by anyone in the Selkirk area.

The Bowhill Estate also runs a riding centre offering pony trekking for beginners, and trail riding for experienced riders, with treks of up to five hours escorted by experienced guides.

Not surprisingly, there is excellent fishing in the Selkirk area. The Ettrick Water offers trout fishing in season (1 April to 30 September), with tickets available for periods from a day up to a month. There is stillwater fishing for brown trout and rainbow trout on Lindean Reservoir during the same months, with 3-rod boats available. In both cases the firm of D. & H. McDonald, 9-11 High Street, Selkirk, will advise and issue permits.

On the A708 not far from Broadmeadows is the hamlet of Foulshiels, the birthplace in 1771 of the noted explorer Mungo Park. He spent much time in Africa, particularly exploring the River Niger, with a spell as a doctor in Peebles between expeditions. He died in Africa in 1806; there is a statue of him in Selkirk High Street.

The A708 continues up the Yarrow Valley, a lovely drive at any time, particularly perhaps in spring, when the many trees are in fresh leaf. This valley was the home ground of James Hogg, a fine poet generally known as the Ettrick Shepherd, who was glorified in verse by Wordsworth. Yarrow Kirk, in the village of that name, dates back to 1640 and is worth a visit.

Passing the Gordon Arms Hotel, an excellent hostelry, the road winds on towards the lovely St Mary's Loch. Up a track running northwards into the hills from the east end of the loch is Dryhope Tower, a typical Border fortification doubling as a dwelling-place. It was the birthplace of Mary Scott, known as 'the flower of Yarrow', who married a noted reiver named Auld Wat of Harden in 1576. Sir Walter Scott is descended from her.

A little east of the Dryhope track, a fine walk leads into the hills from Craig Douglas, part of an old droving track. The way is clear past Blackhouse, with its tower, and on to Muttonhall, following the Douglas Burn the whole time. The return walk is about six miles; and there is an alternative way back south-west across the hill from Blackhouse to join the Dryhope track.

St Mary's Loch must be one of the finest settings for sailing anywhere in Britain; the sailing club is at the west end of the loch, on the neck of land between it and the smaller Loch of the Lowes. Here too is the Tibbie Shiels Inn, which has been giving comfort to travellers for two centuries and more. Tibbie Shiels was a shepherd's wife who ran the inn during the time of Sir Walter Scott, who was a frequent visitor. She died in 1878 at the age of ninety-five. An alternative refreshment-place is a cafe beside the monument to James Hogg, open during the summer months.

The Selkirkshire boundary runs along the ridge on the north side of the Ettrick Valley (described in chapter 3) and round the head of the valley to turn north at Wind Fell. Ettrick Valley is also well worth exploring, with another monument to Hogg at the village of Ettrick. It can be reached on foot through the hills from the south end of Loch of the Lowes — a fine walk of 7 miles or so — but you would need an obliging chauffeur to pick you up. An alternative is to walk from the north end of the same loch by Earls Hill and Hopehouse Burn to Hopehouse, a few miles further down the Ettrick Valley (also about seven miles of walking).

The B7009 winds its way down this beautiful valley back towards Selkirk. In the hills either side are any number of ruined towers, evidence of more unsettled times. They are marked on OS and Bartholomew maps, and many have tracks leading up to them which make fine short walks. Ettrickbridge, about five miles up-valley from the junction of Ettrick and Yarrow, is the home of the present leader of the Liberal party, David Steel, whose constituency is one of the largest in Britain as will be evident

from its name — Roxburgh, Selkirk and Peebles.

It is a beautiful area indeed he has responsibility for, and the discerning visitor will seek out the less well known and remoter attractions, mostly unpublicised, well off the main roads and sometimes hard to reach. I have mentioned Blackhouse Tower, the seat of the Douglas family as far back as the eleventh century, when this was a renowned hunting area. A typical Border story of romance and intrigue is associated with it. The daughter of the house had fallen in love with a neighbouring laird, known to us only as William. The young couple decided to elope, although they must have known that Margaret's father and seven brothers would give chase — as inevitably they did.

In the best tradition of brave lovers, William took them on one at a time and slew them all. Seven stones on the hillside are said to mark their resting places (there seems not to be a stone for the father). William was injured, which is hardly surprising, but he did not tell Margaret of his wounds. They reached St Mary's Loch and stopped for a rest and a drink of the cool water. Then Lady Margaret saw how badly hurt was her swain.

As fast as they could, they rode on to William's home where he was ministered to and put to bed. Alas, his injuries were too severe and he died before morning. Margaret died, too, of a broken heart we must presume, and they were buried together in St Mary's Church by the loch.

Two other towers which can be seen are at Kirkhope and Oakwood. Kirkhope is set up on the hillside north of the village of Ettrick Bridge, and makes an attractive short walk. It was home to the elder sons of the Scotts of Harden, and it was to here that Mary, the Flower of Yarrow, came as bride to Auld Wat.

Oakwood is a tall building now integrated into the farm steading of the same name, a mile or so up the Ettrick Valley from its junction with the Yarrow. It is one of a number of Border houses associated with the wizard Michael Scott. This strange thirteenth-century figure studied at several of the great universities of Europe and was for a time Astrologer Royal to the Emperor Frederick II before returning to England where he was knighted by Edward I.

Shortly before his death he was sent with Sir Michael Wemyss to Norway to bring back to Scotland Margaret, known as the Maid of Norway, who had become heiress to Scotland's throne following the death of Alexander III. Michael Scott died in 1292, and is supposed to have left a mighty book of magic buried somewhere in the grounds of Melrose Abbey.

The south-east corner of Selkirkshire, between the Ettrick Valley and the A7, is little visited, but it contains many fine walks. It is criss-crossed by old tracks, and study of the Ordnance Survey map (1:50,000 sheets no 73 and 79) will reveal plenty of possibilities. Ettrick Bridge to Essenside, or southwards by Shaws Underloch to the Ale Water, or the valley of the Deloraine Burn are just three examples. It is better for the visitor to find them for himself.

From all these walks you can look into our next county, Roxburghshire — to the old towns of Melrose and Hawick, to the new administrative centre of Newtown St Boswells and always to the alluring triple peaks of the Eildon Hills, which dominate the area.

6 Roxburghshire

Roxburgh is one of the four districts that now make up Borders Region. Its modern boundaries are slightly different from those of the old shire, which I am following in this chapter. Our first stopping place, Melrose, is nowadays in the district of Ettrick and Lauderdale, but it is, just, a Roxburghshire town and it makes a worthy introduction to this chapter.

Melrose is small, with a population of only 2,000, but it is a very ancient settlement and its history is as rich as any place in Scotland. There is evidence that a chapel dedicated to St Cuthbert was here in the seventh century, and long before that the Romans were occupying the slopes of the Eildon Hills at their fort called *Trimontium*.

The heart and centre-piece of Melrose is the great Abbey, a Cistercian foundation in 1136 in the reign of David I. It suffered repeatedly at the hands of English invading armies — pillaged and burnt by Edward II in 1322; virtually destroyed again by Richard II in 1385; and burnt yet again in the infamous 'rough wooing' of Henry VIII, in 1546.

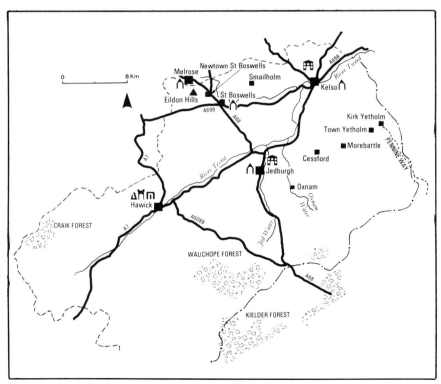

Melrose Abbey

Despite this, much remains, and the stonework is magnificent — tracery and flying buttresses in a reddish stone, with the highlight of it all perhaps the window in the north transept with its famous 'crown of thorns'.

There are some extraordinary examples of carving and statuary — a pig playing the bagpipes and a Virgin Mary with headless child among them. It is said that the head of the child fell on the arm of a man trying to demolish the statue during the Reformation, crippling him for life. Another piece depicts a mason with his chisel and mallet. The Abbey is full of wonderful stories, many of them in the guide available at the entrance. One I particularly like is that of Robert the Bruce, who was so grieved at the Abbey's desecration in 1322 that he voted the enormous sum (for those days) of £2,000 for its restoration. The snag was that there was rather less than this amount in the entire Scots treasury! The restoration was nonetheless carried out, though perhaps over a longer period of time than the king would have wished.

Robert Bruce has a further association with Melrose Abbey — his heart is buried here, its final resting place after long travels around Europe in a lead casket, during the Crusades. In the side chapels are burial places for notable Border families, including Scotts, Pringles and Douglases. Melrose Abbey is in the care of the Secretary of State for Scotland and is open all year.

Alongside the Abbey, and certainly not to be missed, is the splendid Priorwood Garden, owned by the National Trust for Scotland since 1974. The garden specialises in plants that can be dried for display, and a selection of dried flowers, with pamphlets on how to use and prepare them, is always on sale at the shop. There is an orchard with a special 'Apples through the Ages' walk, and a picnic area. Priorwood is open from 1 April to Christmas, and admission is free, with a donation box in the garden. Each autumn a special sale of dried plants is held to raise money for the Trust.

The Borders Information Centre adjoins Priorwood, and staff here will be glad to help with any enquiries you may have regarding places of interest in the area, accommodation, food, etc. A wide range of tourist literature is available. For the active visitor, as well as many walks, some of which I shall describe later, there is a 9-hole golf course in a charming setting, and fishing on the Tweed for salmon, brown and sea trout. Information is available from Anglers Choice in High Street, and there is an unusual beat between Gattonside House and the Suspension Bridge; unusual in that it is controlled by the monks at St Aidans, Gattonside. There is no set fee; like the other Melrose beats, this is fly fishing only, with a limited number of rods, and a donation is asked to go to St Aidans' work with the mentally handicapped.

Melrose, not unnaturally, has its own festival and riding, held in mid-June. The principal, a bachelor of the town, is called the Melrosian and his 'kirking' on a Sunday morning marks the Festival's opening. Later that day there is a gym-khana with showjumping and other events in Gibson Park, the presentations being made by the Melrosian's mother.

The main ride takes place on Monday evening; starting from Greenyards, the procession crosses the Tweed, climbs the Eildon Hills, back over the river, up to Gattonside Heights, and finally back to the town, where the Melrosian is pre-sented with a riding crop and prizes are awarded to the oldest rider, the youngest, and the smartest turnout.

Thursday sees the crowning of the Festival Queen — the Dux or Head Girl of Melrose Grammar School — in the Abbey, and on Saturday the principals tour the district (by coach now, although it would have been on horseback in times past) before the final sports in the afternoon. These include the Eildon Hill Race, entered each year by leading fell runners from many parts of Britain and an exciting spectacle.

We cannot leave Melrose without mentioning the Rugby club and its famous seven-a-side tournament, held in April each year. Competition over the long day is fierce but fair, and there is always a great turnout for a splendid sporting occasion. Never more so than in April 1983, when the tournament was due to celebrate its centenary with a special invitation event and international teams taking part.

Although there is plenty of celebration at and after the Melrose Sevens, it is perhaps a slightly more peaceful occasion than its antecedent, the game of Handba'. Played on Fastern's Eve in February it involved virtually the entire active male population of the town. The ball, a leather bag stuffed with a bullock's bladder, was thrown into the air at the old Market Cross at one o'clock in the afternoon, and the game (often more like a war!) began. There seem to have been no rules, and it all carried on until exhaustion and darkness overtook the players. The game was banned by Melrose Town Council in 1901.

A short walk northwards from the Abbey to the Tweed leads to the Chain Bridge linking the town with Gattonside. It was one of the first suspension bridges in Scotland, opened in October 1826; no more than eight people may be on it at any one time and it is an offence to make the bridge rock or swing. The

PLACES TO VISIT AROUND MELROSE

Melrose Abbey
Twelfth-century Cistercian foundation, now a wonderfully evocative ruin.

Priorwood Garden (National Trust for Scotland)
Specialises in plants that can be dried for display. Shop.

Chain Bridge
Very early suspension bridge, 1826.

Eildon Hills
Historical walk with superb views.

Dryburgh Abbey
Twelfth/thirteenth-century ruins, fine cloisterhouse. Grave of Sir Walter Scott and Earl Haig.

Bemersyde
Home of the Haig family.

Smailholm Tower
One of the most impressive Border towers, on a rocky knoll.

riverside path on the south bank leads to Melrose Cauld, a rapid stretch of water made by the Abbey monks to take water to their mill lade. A path leads on up to Weir Hill, with a fine view along the Tweed.

North again from here, up the valley of the Allan Water, are two more of the Border towers, at Glendearg and Langshaw. 'Glendearg', an odd name for this area, is in fact an invention of Sir Walter Scott's, used in his book *The Monastery*.

The true name of the place is Hillslap, but it is marked as Glendearg on all modern maps and the old name is almost forgotten. The tower, an L-shaped sixteenth-century building, can be seen by asking at the farm.

Just east of Melrose is Newstead, reputed to be the oldest continually inhabited village in Scotland. It lies on part of the site of the Roman fort of *Trimontium* and has been occupied ever since. The Romans are believed to have built a bridge over the Tweed here to carry Dere Street on towards Edinburgh. There is now little direct evidence of *Trimontium,* as the excavations were efficiently covered over, though there is a memorial in the form of an altar on the road from Newstead to Leaderfoot.

Before leaving the Melrose area, I hope you will have time to take a walk on the Eildon Hills. The highest point is only 1,385ft (420m) but they dominate the area; truly they are the jewel at the centre of the Borders. The Eildons have a long history and are rich in legend. Taking the latter first, it is said that King Arthur is buried here (one of many places in Britain carrying this legend) and that the wizard Michael Scott clove them into three.

It's a nice story, but, alas, untrue. The Eildons were formed from volcanic activity millions of years ago; geologically they are a cluster of domes of plutonic rock standing above the old red sandstone, which can clearly be seen in the colour of the soil around Jedburgh in particular. They have undoubtedly been three hills for many thousands of years.

There is a signposted walk, called the Eildon Walk, starting from the square in Melrose. It is about four miles in length and on a clear day gives wonderful views. Walk along Dingleton Road for

Eildon Hills, near Melrose

about 200 yards to the signpost, where you turn left and start a fairly steep climb, heading towards Eildon Hill North. At the top hedge, go half right, climbing towards the col between Hill North and Middle Hill. The latter is the highest of the three and is an easy climb. On its summit are a triangulation pillar and a mountain indicator — a brass plate inscribed with the names of many of the hills and points of interest. The indicator was erected in 1927 and was paid for by public subscription. It bears the dedication: 'To the memory of Sir Walter Scott. From this spot he was wont to view and point the glories of the Borderland'. Take your time and view them too.

If you wish to make the short diversion to Wester Hill you may do so before returning over Mid Hill to go on to the summit of Hill North. Here was sited an Iron Age hill fort, extending to 39 acres at its peak. It must be remembered that at that time the hilltops would have risen above a dense forest covering most of the lower ground and would therefore have given a very commanding position.

You may be able to see the lines of defence on the ground, with their gateways, and also a number of small mounds which mark the sites of huts occupied at the time the hill fort was built. No fewer than 296 of these hut sites have been discovered, together with some pottery which must have been used by the inhabitants. The only inhabitants now may be birds; the area has a richly varied fauna including pipits, snipe, grouse, skylarks, and other rarer varieties.

The view of the Cheviot Hills from here is particularly fine. After enjoying it to the full, take the path leading east and then north to the top of Eildontree Plantation, where it meets the path encircling the hill on its northern flank.

You now drop downhill quite steeply; part of this route is used by horses as well as people, and can be muddy at times.

The signposted route turns right at the road and left in a short while, going down to Newstead. A diversion to the right take you to the site of Trimontium; straight ahead leads to the Tweed and a very pleasant riverside walk back into Melrose; or you can turn left for a more direct route to the town. Whichever way you choose to end your walk, if the conditions have been fair I am sure you will have found it very satisfying. It should also have made you eager to explore the surrounding Borders countryside. We can best do that by moving on to the next town east from Melrose, Newtown St Boswells, and neighbouring Dryburgh with the second of the Border Abbeys.

Before finally leaving the Eildon Hills you might like to note that a detailed guide to the area is published by the Scottish Wildlife Trust and available from local shops or from the Hon Secretary of the Tweed Valley Branch, Mr Michael Braithwaite, Cockspurs, Lilliesleaf, Roxburghshire.

We are heading for the next Borders abbey, Dryburgh; an interesting way of getting there is to take the back road, B6359, south for Bowden out of Melrose. Bowden is a pretty village with a green and an old church which still retains the 'laird's loft' where the lord of the manor and his family would sit during services. At one time this was a weaving village, but the coming of mills and machinery to the surrounding towns led to the demise of this true cottage industry.

The road to Bowden gives fine 'backside' views of the Eildon Hills; turn left out of the village on B6398 to keep those views as far as Newtown St Boswells, where the headquarters of the Borders Regional Council is situated. A short mile down the A68 from here is the older village of St Boswells, actually named after an early Christian saint called Boisil, one of the first missionaries to reach Lowland Scotland. The village has a very fine tree-ringed green where cricket is played in the summer months. It is also the scene of a gipsy fair in July each year. The gipsies now come in cars and modern caravans rather than the horse-drawn variety, but the scene is still as colourful and you can have your fortune told if you wish.

It is possible to drive to Dryburgh from St Boswells but it is much more pleasant to approach the abbey on foot from the village, crossing the Tweed by a footbridge. Dryburgh was the second Border abbey to be established, not long after Melrose, and being away from any towns or main roads it has a marvellously peaceful atmosphere. Most of the existing remains date from the twelfth or thirteenth century, and the cloister buildings are still complete enough for us to imagine what the abbey was like when it was in daily use. Sir Walter Scott and Field Marshal Earl Haig are both

Dryburgh Abbey

buried here, and the abbey is open to view all year round. There is an admission charge.

Further pleasant exercise can be gained by following a riverside walk maintained by the regional council. The walk, about four miles in length, starts in Newtown St Boswells by the Post Office. Walk down Melbourne Place and

Smailholm Tower

look for the signpost on the left saying 'To the Glen'. This road changes to a track and leads to a small footbridge over a burn. The path leads on to the Tweed by the footbridge to Dryburgh. Do not cross the river but keep on the south bank.

Stay by the river until the path leaves it to go up to St Boswells. Follow the

path up this little valley, cross the burn and walk back down the other side to reach the riverside golf course (9-hole, open to visitors). The path stays by the river all the way to Mertoun Bridge; go over the B6404 and carry on to a stile which leads into a wood near Benrig House.

Climb some steps beside a wall and follow the path left beside the graveyard; it eventually climbs again through a wood to Maxton Church. There is a postbus back to Newtown from Maxton village, except on Sundays.

There are two more places to visit before we move on towards Kelso. The first is cheating a little, for it is just over the county boundary into Berwickshire, but it is far more logical to include it here. On B6356 between Dryburgh and Earlston is the great house of Bemersyde, the home of the Haig family for centuries. It was bought by the nation after World War I and given to the great soldier, who lived there until his death. His son, now in residence, is a serious painter whose work has been exhibited in galleries in Scotland, London and New York. Another branch of the family founded the well-known whisky distilling firm, and the former American Secretary of State, Alexander Haig, is also related. The house is open to the public at certain times.

Close to Bemersyde is 'Scott's View', a point where the writer often stopped his carriage to admire the panorama over the Tweed to the Eildon Hills. His horses got so accustomed to stopping there that on his last voyage of all, to be buried at Dryburgh, they stopped automatically at this point. A little nearer to Dryburgh, another notable Scotsman, William Wallace, is commemorated by a 21-foot statue just off the road. The statue was commissioned by the 11th Earl of Buchan, and was completed in 1814.

A little north of Bemersyde, a minor road leads east to the village of Smailholm (and back into Roxburghshire). This has a small church with a Scott Memorial Window, but the main attraction is a couple of miles away at the steading of Sandyknowe. It is Smailholm Tower, an outstanding example of its type, set on a rocky knoll. The tower is 57ft high and in a good state of preservation. This might not have been the case, for in 1799 the tower was due to be demolished.

Sir Walter Scott heard of the plans and pleaded with the owner to change his mind. Scott had spent many happy days at Sandyknowe as a small boy — his grandparents had the farm. He loved the place and there is no doubt it was the inspiration for many of his works. He could not bear to think of the tower being demolished, and his pleas must have been eloquent, for the owner, Scott of Harden, agreed to stay his hand, provided Sir Walter wrote a ballad about Smailholm. The result was *Eve of Saint John*, a romance of love, murder and revenge. Smailholm is open all the year round, free of charge.

Following the road from Smailholm to Kelso will lead to the entrance to Floors Castle, home of the Duke and Duchess of Roxburghe and one of the great houses of the Borders. The house was built in 1721 by William Adam for the 1st Duke, on the site of an earlier building, and commands glorious views of the Tweed Valley and the distant Cheviots. The house has a roofscape as exotic as any in Britain, with fretting, corner towers and balustrades. Old maps show the name as 'Fleurs', French for flowers, and indeed Floors (or Fleurs) has been famous for its carnations for many years. The present walled garden, a little way west of the house, produces all the flowers, fruit and

---

PLACES TO VISIT AROUND KELSO

Floors Castle
Adam house, home of the Duke of Roxburghe. Fine French furniture, collection of stuffed birds, gardens.

Kelso Abbey
Impressive ruin, attacked many times. Burial place of Dukes of Roxburghe.

Old Parish Church, Kelso
Unusual octagonal shape.

Kelso Bridge
Designed by John Rennie and used as a model for Waterloo Bridge in London.

Turret House
Seventeenth-century town house used in summer as the Tourist Information Centre.

Thomson Monument, Ednam
Tower erected to the poet's memory on Ferny Hill.

---

vegetables for the estate including such exotic varieties as melons, peaches and nectarines. There is a garden centre, opened in 1978, where produce and plants can be bought. A holly tree in the park is said to mark the spot where King James II of Scotland was accidentally killed by a bursting cannon in 1460. Floors Castle itself contains an outstanding collection of French furniture from the seventeenth and eighteenth centuries, many fine paintings, and tapestries. More unusual exhibits include a fine collection of stuffed birds, including now extinct species such as the passenger pigeon, and (in the basement) a model of the castle made from matchsticks and icing sugar. It was made by a castle chef in 1851. The basement also contains a facsimile of the Kelso Charter, a superbly illuminated manuscript which granted lands to Benedictine monks. The original is on loan to the National Library of Edinburgh. Also on display is a letter written by Mary Queen of Scots in September 1566 summoning the Laird of Cessford to discuss a visit to Jedburgh.

Floors Castle is open over the Easter weekend and then from the beginning of May to late September. The gardens and garden centre are open all year. Pipe bands play on a number of occasions during the summer.

So we come to Kelso, perfectly set at the junction of Teviot and Tweed and described by Scott as 'the most beautiful town in Scotland'. It is a busy market town with a population of around 5,000, and nowadays also hosts a number of firms manufacturing electronic equipment. Pride of the town is the Abbey, established in 1128 when the name appears to have been 'Calchou'. At this

Kelso

time the town, set on the south bank of the river, was called Roxburgh, with a fine castle on the Marchmount. Who held Marchmount, held the entrance to Scotland, it is said. It changed hands many times in the years between the twelfth and mid-seventeenth century; now there is virtually no trace of town or castle left.

The Abbey survives, hardly intact, but still giving a real impression of grandeur. It was attacked innumerable times in the sixteenth century, notably in the 'rough wooing' of 1545 and by the Reformers in 1560. By 1587 it was reduced to the remnant we see today; since that time it has been in the hands of the Dukes of Roxburghe.

The main remnant is the western transept, which served as the parish church until 1771, when a fall of part of the roof (which had only been added in 1649) caused it to be abandoned. The arcade on the south side of the abbey is the burial place of the Dukes of Roxburghe; although this was not built until 1933, it does include a thirteenth-century ornamented doorway and a window of stained glass which is much older.

Behind the Abbey is the Old Parish Church, designed in an octagonal shape by local architect James Nisbet — he was perhaps following the advice of John Wesley, who maintained that an octagon was the best shape for a preacher to use. Behind the church in turn is the passageway known as the Butts, where bowmen used to practise their skills — Border archers were renowned for their accuracy in the Middle Ages.

On a bend of the Tweed is the fine bridge designed by John Rennie and built in 1803 to succeed an older structure swept away by floods. The present bridge has itself survived a number of notable floods, the most recent being in 1977 when the water level was 12ft above normal. Rennie used the Kelso bridge as a model for Waterloo Bridge in London, and when that was demolished in 1935, two of its elegant lamps were brought to Kelso to stand at the south end of the bridge over the Tweed after shining down on the Thames for over 100 years.

The oldest surviving house in Kelso is in Abbey Row, not far from the bridge. It is Turret House, a seventeenth-century building that has been carefully restored and is used in the summer as a Tourist Information Centre. At the other end of Horsemarket and Woodmarket is the Square, with fine eighteenth- and nineteenth-century town houses, and the Town Hall, built in 1816 with funds provided by the people of Kelso. At one time the bell here rang at six in the morning to rouse the people for work and again at eight in the evening, when their labours could cease. Perhaps we are not too badly off these days?

The Bull Ring, in the centre of the square, is just what it says — the point where bulls were tethered during markets. Markets, and shows, are now held in Springwood Park, across the river. There are three important shows in the month of July — Kelso Ram Sales, the biggest in Scotland; the Ponies of Britain show: and the Border Union Show, which for livestock and produce is second only to the Royal Highland Show itself.

Other sporting occasions include horse races at various times at Berrymoss, on the north edge of the town, point-to-point meetings based at Friarshaugh in February and March, and cricket in Shedden Park — Kelso Cricket Club was the first to be formed in Scotland, in 1821, and is still going strong.

Kelso Civic Week is also held in July, and includes the ceremonies and rideouts presided over by the Kelso Laddie. The main rideouts are on the Friday (the Whipman's Ride) and on the Saturday, when the riders go all the way to Yetholm, practically on the border. The Laddie and his Right Hand and Left Hand Men actually go to the border, where he picks three sprigs from a fir tree for their lapels. On their return to Kirk Yetholm Green he is presented with the Yetholm Dagger — a nasty-looking piece of work, the favoured weapon of the gipsies in earlier times.

I should have explained that the Kelso Laddie is also the Whipman; his installation in this office takes place on the Friday evening of Festival Week in the Square. His Lass busses the town flag, and he then leads his followers to the supposed site of the Trysting Tree where he carves his initials in the ground. On both Friday and Saturday evening there are parades and other social occasions.

There is a pleasant signposted walk along the River Teviot from Kelso to Kalemouth, a distance of about six miles. It can be started from the Kelso Bridge or from the ruins of Roxburgh Castle; on its way it passes through the modern Roxburgh village, a small place with a rather more peaceful history than its predecessor. There is a bus service (Eastern 420) back from Kalemouth, or you can use it to get there and then walk back to Kelso if you prefer.

Two miles north of Kelso is the village of Ednam, associated with two writers. The poet James Thomson (1700-1748) is commemorated by a monument on Ferny Hill; he wrote the words of *Rule Britannia* and many other works, including the major four-part *Seasons.* Henry France Lyte's words are often sung on Sundays throughout the land; he was a hymn-writer whose works include *Abide With Me* and *Praise, my Soul, the King of Heaven* and his life (1793-1847) is marked by a plaque on Ednam Bridge (one of the gathering points, incidentally, for the 1715 Rising).

Turning south, take the A698 to the village of Crailing, with its ancient Market Cross, and turn right for Nisbet, beautifully sited among woods and below the slopes of Peniel Heugh. There were once several towers here, but no trace of them remains. Peniel Heugh is the site of the Wellington Monument, and is part of a most interesting estate with a tremendous range of activities for the visitor.

Lothian Estates have set up here a 'Conservation Concept' with a Woodland Centre entered from the A68 near its junction with B6400, west of Nisbet. The Centre is open from Easter to the end of October and features an exhibition related to trees, woodwork and natural history — the theme changes from time to time. Slide/tape programmes on local conservation and nature themes can be seen, there is a large play area for children, and board games in two guises. A 'quiet room' offers tables for backgammon, chess and cribbage and giant boards can be used in another part of the Centre to play Nine Men's Morris, draughts, etc. Rules for all games are available, and your family or group can stage a competition.

Refreshment facilities are naturally available, and you may wish to make use of these after taking one of several fine woodland walks laid out on the estate. The Roman Road Walk is about $2\frac{1}{2}$ miles and, as the name implies, leads to a section of Dere Street. Cricket Park Walk is a straightforward mile circuit of the park. The Doocot Walk, $2\frac{1}{2}$ miles, leads down to the river and the doocot itself, a 20-foot diameter structure holding stone nesting boxes for pigeons.

The longest walk on the estate is the Wellington Walk, of about three miles. leading up to the monument on Peniel Heugh. This was started within two weeks of the Battle of Waterloo in June 1815, though the wooden top dates from 1867. The monument is 150ft high and there are 228 steps in a spiral staircase giving access to the viewing gallery. The tower can be climbed *only* by escorted parties — ask at the Woodland Centre for details.

Even if you cannot climb the tower, there is still a superb view from the hill, with the Eildon Hills and the Cheviots standing out on a clear day. The monument was built by the 6th Marquess of Lothian and the present holder of the title still has his home at Monteviot House on the estate. The house was started in 1740 and has been added to a number of times. It is open on Wednesday afternoons in the summer.

The whole estate is geared to visitors, while still remaining a working estate. A fascinating place where you could easily spend a whole day; adults can browse in the excellent bookshop while the children enjoy a slice of Woodland Cake in the tearoom. The literature says it is 'guaranteed to satisfy the hungriest child' — now *there's* a challenge!

So we come to Jedburgh, a town with a thousand years of history behind it; but although it takes care of the relics of its past, it lives firmly in the present and there are a number of light industrial sites. Jedburgh's pride is the Abbey, miraculously well preserved in view of its extremely turbulent history.

It was founded, as were the other Border Abbeys, by David I, in 1138, as an Augustinian Priory. The first Abbey was not completed until 1227, and over the next 330 years it was destroyed to some extent no less than eight times,

PLACES TO VISIT AROUND JEDBURGH

Lothian Estates Woodland Centre, Monteviot
Visitor centre, board games, woodland walks, displays. Peniel Heugh monument. Monteviot House open at limited times.

Jedburgh Abbey
Founded 1138 as Augustinian Priory. Superb setting overlooking River Jed.

Castle Jail, Jedburgh
Museum of local and social history.

Mary Queen of Scots House, Jedburgh
Sixteenth-century town house now restored, with mementoes of Mary and her period.

Leyden Memorial, Denholm
Commemorates life of scholar and minister.

rebuilt each time, and finally abandoned after the harrowing raids of 1545. The earliest parts to have survived are at the east end. There is a fine rose window, and the north transept serves as the burial vault for the family of the Marquesses of Lothian.

From the Abbey, with its superb outlook over a bend of Jed Water, it is a short step up to Castlegate and the Castle Jail, built in 1823 to a castellated design by Archibald Eliot, and now serving as a museum of local and social history, well worth a visit.

Prince Charlie stayed in a house in Castlegate, at the corner of Blackhills Close, on his way south in 1745 — his

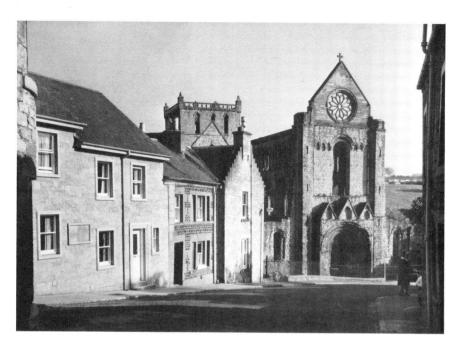

Jedburgh Close and Abbey

last stopping place in Scotland before crossing the Border on the ill-fated march to Derby. The exterior of the house has been restored. Two hundred years earlier, another fated figure from Scots history stayed in Jedburgh. Mary was a bonny lass of twenty-three when she came here, as Queen, to hold a Circuit Court in 1566. The country was still simmering with plots, in some of which she was a central character. Although Mary was married to Lord Darnley, she left Jedburgh on a wild ride to Hermitage Castle to see the injured Earl of Bothwell. The weather was appalling, and the return was accomplished within the day — 50 miles ridden and only 2 hours spent at Hermitage. Mary contracted a fever from which she nearly died.

While in Jedburgh Mary stayed at a fortified 'Bastle House' which now serves as a museum illustrating the living conditions of the time. Mary's bedroom can be seen, and there are some valuable relics in the Great Hall.

Jedburgh is pronounced 'Jethart' by the inhabitants, and its Festival bears this name, the Jethart Callants; it is held at the beginning of July and lasts for two weeks. After a short rideout to Southdean on the opening Saturday, the first main event is on the Monday when the Callant leads a ride to Morebattle for a meeting with the Kelso Laddie. Thursday sees another local ride, to Crailing, and on the middle Saturday of the Festival the main and longest ride, to Redeswire on the Border itself, takes place. A guest speaker is traditionally invited to give an address at the site of the battle at Redeswire, after which the return ride passes through Oxnam and Falla, where races take place. All those

69

Mary Queen of Scots house, Jedburgh

completing this ride for the first time receive a badge on their return.

On the second Monday the ride follows part of Mary's route to Hermitage; on Tuesday the riders go to Lanton for a Gymkhana; and on Wednesday Ancrum is the destination, where the Callant's Reel is danced. On the Thursday the Callant takes custody of the Jedburgh flag and the Friday is a day full of colour and pageantry. The Callant's Cavalcade visits Ferniehirst Castle and returns via Douglas Camp and the ancient Capon Tree for a ceremonial return to Jedburgh at the

War Memorial. In the evening the Callant's Ball is held. On the final Saturday the Jedburgh Games round off the Festival in great style.

There are several places of interest between Jedburgh and Hawick. Denholm has as its centre-piece the memorial to Dr John Leyden (1775-1811) who packed an impressive list of achievements into a short life. He was a shepherd's son but qualified as both a doctor and a minister before his study of Oriental languages took him to India and Malaya. He held office as a professor of languages in Bengal and

70

served under Lord Minto in Calcutta before dying of fever in Java aged thirty-six. His thatched cottage birthplace is in the village; another fine Denholm building is Westgate Hall, with its lintel dated 1663.

Minto has been mentioned; the village and hills after which the Earldom was named is just north of Denholm. Several Earls of Minto (Elliots by birth) served with distinction in colonial offices, the fourth Earl being Viceroy of India in the early years of the twentieth century. Minto House was the birthplace of Jean Elliot (1727-1805) who wrote a set of words for the pipe lament *The Flowers of the Forest*.

South of Denholm is Rubers Law, a fine viewpoint easily reached from the village, firstly along lanes, and then by a clear track up the north ridge of the hill. Although only 1,400ft (424m) it commands an impressive spread of country and the round trip of about five miles is well worth doing on a clear day.

Bedrule, on a minor road east of Denholm, has both old and new claims to fame despite its small size. In the Middle Ages there was a castle here, a Turnbull stronghold from where the fierce clan controlled the surrounding country. The castle was sited not far from the point where the modern church with its splendid heraldic ceiling now stands. Bedrule is the home of the Leadbetter stable of racing horses, and the 1979 Grand National winner, Rubstic, came from this stable.

As might be expected from the second part of its name, Bonchester Bridge has Roman connections. There was a fort on Bonchester Hill, on one of the routes north from the crossing at Carter Bar. Brown trout fishing is available on the Rule Water — permits from the Horse and Hounds Inn, in the village. If bowls is your game you can be sure of a comfortable session in Bonchester — an all-weather green has been set up here and is a popular attraction.

From Bonchester Bridge, the A6088 winds a twisty 7 miles north-west to join the A7 2 miles east of Hawick, the largest of the Border burghs with a population of about 17,000. It is the administrative centre for the modern Roxburgh District. Hawick has an interest in beasts alive and dead; it has the longest-established auction mart in Britain, with several hundred thousand sheep and cattle passing through each year, and has been a knitwear centre for as long, with a reputation for both clothing and carpets.

Hawick today provides an excellent range of facilities for the visitor. There is an 18-hole golf course on Vertish Hill, a modern swimmng pool and leisure centre, and in the beautiful 107-acre Wilton Lodge Park you can enjoy tennis, bowls, putting, or work out on the Jubilee Trim Track, opened in 1978. Or of course you can simply stroll among the many fine trees or sit by the riverside watching others at play. Wilton Lodge itself contains a very well run museum giving a full picture of Border life, social, industrial and archaeo-logical; and the Scott Gallery hosts travelling exhibitions of art, changing frequently.

From the west end of the park, where Langlands Bridge — preserving the name of former owners of the Lodge — crosses the River Teviot, it is a pleasant riverside stroll back into town, reaching the Tourist Information Centre in Common Haugh. Recrossing the river leads you to St Mary's Church, rebuilt in 1764 on a grassy knoll above the Slitrig stream. There was a strange flood along here in 1767. The Teviot ran at its usual level, but in the space of only two hours, the Slitrig rose over twenty feet and carried away fifteen houses and a mill. Fortunately no-one was killed. The flood is said to have been caused by fairies who lived in a pool at the source of the stream, high on Wyndburgh Hill, and were angered by a shepherd throwing stones into their mountain home. So be careful not to do likewise!

Further out along the Slitrig is the Motte, still something of a mystery. A conical mound about twenty-five feet high, it might be the base for a Norman fortification, or be much older. No-one knows for sure. Moat Park surrounds the Motte and is another enjoyable place to visit.

The Motte features in the ceremonies of the Hawick Common Riding, as does the impressive equestrian statue at the north end of High Street. It commemorates the Hornshole Raid of 1514, when Hawick youths partly redeemed the awful tragedy of Flodden by routing a band of English raiders and taking their flag back to Hawick. The Hawick Cornet bears a flag in exactly the same style — blue with a gold cross — during the Common Riding, which with all its rideouts lasts for over a month. There are rideouts each Saturday in May, to Bonchester Bridge, Lilliesleaf, Robertson, Mosspaul, and finally to Denholm, with shorter rides in midweek. Of all these, Mosspaul is the principal. It is a long day indeed, reaching the Border at the Mosspaul Inn via Skelfhill and Millstone Edge.

The main Common Riding ceremonies and events take place on the first or second weekend in June. Things start to move on the Thursday evening, when the Cornet's Lass busses the flag by tying blue and gold ribbons to its staff. This, the only part of the ceremonies involving ladies, is held in the Town Hall, and tickets are allocated by ballot, so great is the demand. After the bussing, the Cornet's Walk takes its way through the town to the statue, where the flag on the monument is bussed.

Friday morning at 6am sees the drum and fife band parading round the town to the Auld Brig, and in the morning the races known as Cornet's Chase are held at Nipknowes. Riders are divided into married and unmarried classes. Following this, riders make for Pilmuir where the Cornet cuts a ceremonial piece of turf, a symbol of pasture and tillage. The horsemen then gallop round the moor to the racecourse for more races.

After racing ends, the Cornet with his two main supporters takes the flag to the Coble Pool on the Teviot and dips it three times to warn intruders that they may come to this point but no further. There is little rest for the Cornet; in the evening he has a dinner and ball which

---

PLACES TO VISIT AROUND HAWICK

Wilton Lodge Park, Hawick
Riverside walks, trim track, museum of Border life, art gallery.

The Motte
Conical mound believed to be base of ancient fortification.

Branxholme Castle
Border tower, setting for Scott's *Lay of the Last Minstrel.*

Riddell Monument, Teviothead
Commemorates Henry Scott Riddell, poet and minister.

Linton Church
Built on a hillock of pure sand; associated with legend of the 'Linton Worm'.

goes on until the small hours, and he has to be up at dawn to climb the Motte.

Before long the town is again echoing to the sound of fife and drum, leading the principals to Wilton Lodge Park, where a wreath is laid on the war memorial. Then it's more racing, and general sports in the Volunteer Park. At the end of the day the Cornet returns the flag to the Provost and the Common Riding is over.

Riders visiting Hawick for the festivities, or indeed at other times, might like to try the Hawick Circular, a 27-mile horse riding route using minor roads, tracks, and cross country sections. The route has been prepared to take full advantage of the glorious countryside around the town, and passage for riders has been made as easy as possible. The route makes a grand circuit round the old town, and it is interesting to note that half of its route is on land owned by Buccleuch Estates. A leaflet describing the route is available locally.

The route does not quite reach as far out as The Snoot, a beautifully-sited youth hostel on the Borthwick Water 6 miles west of Hawick. From here the Scottish Youth Hostels Association run pony-trekking courses in the summer months, and it is also an excellent base for walkers — or indeed for fishermen, for a couple of miles further west again is Alemoor Loch, where brown trout can be fished in season (mid-March to early October). Permits can be obtained from several shops in Hawick. The smaller and more remote Hellmoor Loch can also be fished, as of course can the rivers in the area.

We could not leave Hawick without mentioning the 'Greens' — the famous rugby club based at Mansfield Park. They have supplied many Scottish internationals, and in common with other Border clubs have a seven-a-side

tournament in the spring. Perhaps it could be said that they continue, on the field of sport, the spirit encompassed in Hawick's battle cry:

Teribus, ye Teri Odin
Sons of heroes slain at Flodden
Imitating Border bowmen
Aye defend your rights in common

Hawick folk are still known as Teries and still defend their rights with passion.

Roxburghshire extends a good way south and west of Hawick, and the A7 follows the Teviot almost to the watershed. Three miles out of the town is Branxholme Castle, which was the principal setting for Scott's *Lay of the Last Minstrel,* a lyrical work of great romantic power. It is still used as a private residence. Further upstream is the village of Teviothead, where Johnnie Armstrong lies buried. He was a renowned reiver and in 1530 was convicted of theft of cattle and ordered by James V to be hanged. Many songs and ballads commemorate him; the astronaut Neil Armstrong is a present-day descendant of another branch of the family. On the hill slopes west of Teviothead is the Riddell Monument, to the memory of Henry Scott Riddell (1798-1870). He was the minister at Teviothead and was renowned locally for his poetry. He, too, is buried in the churchyard here.

The monument makes a pleasant short walk, and there are numerous tracks either side of the Teviot valley leading up into the hills. One of them leads west to the village of Craik, a distance of about seven miles. The area has been extensively planted by the Forestry Commission, and a 3-mile forest walk starts from a picnic place beside the Borthwick Water at Craik. It leads to a waterfall at Wolfcleuchhead, where seats are provided for a rest before you return to your starting point. Pony trekking is also available — enquire locally or at the forest office.

We must now swing east and north on our way through the extensive tract of country between the towns and the Border. First point of call is Hermitage Castle, a superbly evocative place now in the care of the Ancient Monuments Division, and open all year. The castle was a stronghold of the de Soulis family in the thirteenth and fourteenth centuries and then of the Douglases. Mary Queen of Scots rode here from Jedburgh in 1566 to meet Bothwell, an exhausting return ride of 50 miles which nearly led to her death from a fever. The name arises from a monk, Brother William, who retired here to live a life of prayer in the twelfth century. The foundations of the chapel he founded can be seen near the castle.

Hermitage Castle is on the B6399, a splendid route into or out of Scotland if you have plenty of time — it is a narrow, twisty road and cannot be hurried. It is crossed at Roberts Linn Bridge by the Catrail, an earthwork dating from the Dark Ages. It can be walked from Roberts Linn to the minor road at Priesthaugh, a long 10 miles, but you will need to be met at the far end.

At the east side of the extensive Wauchope Forest is Souden Kirk, on the A6088 road from Carter Bar to Hawick. It was excavated in 1910 and is dedicated to the memory of the Scots dead from the battle of Otterburn in 1388 (the battle the English call Chevy Chase, when Hotspur was routed by Douglas, who himself died in victory). An annual service of remembrance is held here. From the kirk it is a short but steep walk to Southdean Law, with a prehistoric fort and settlement on its summit and a fine view as well.

The next road east is the A68, and on

its way to Jedburgh it passes near Ferniehirst Castle, now a youth hostel, but with a long and troubled history. It changed hands several times in the sixteenth century, from the Kers to Lord Dacre, then to the English in 1547, and back to the Scots after a bloody slaughter involving French troops on the Scottish side in 1549. In 1570 it was ruined by the Earl of Sussex in another English raid. Rebuilt, it gives hospitality to visitors from many lands. It is a most unusual hostel with its magnificent staircases and great hall with a vast fireplace.

Not far from the hostel is Ferniehirst Mill Lodge, a centre for riding holidays. The riding here is not for beginners, but the standard of care of both people and horses is very high. In the summer months a 5-day Cheviot Trail Ride covers 100 miles; the horses stay at hill farms overnight while riders are ferried back to base.

East of Ferniehirst is the pretty village of Oxnam, with an attractive white-washed church and a pottery where visitors can watch Peter Holland — the seventh generation of his family to follow this calling —making domestic and ornamental pots and earthenware, and perhaps leave with a souvenir.

The back road from Oxnam to Hownam is crossed by the Roman Dere Street, which can be walked from here to the camp at Chew Green, just into England. There are plans to turn this into a waymarked path linking the Pennine Way with the Southern Upland Way at Selkirk, a stretch of 25 miles through fine rolling country. Hownam is on the Kale Water, and much further up that stream, on Dere Street, is Woden Law. On its summit was a native fort guarding the border; it was overrun and demolished by the Roman army under Agricola in 80AD, after which the Romans themselves built fortifications

Ferniehirst Castle, now a Youth Hostel

here, which it is believed were used largely for siege warfare training.

The back road from Hownam to Woden Law is part of an ancient highway known as The Street or Clattering Path. It too can be walked to the camp at Chew Green, but take care not to cross to the south side of the Coquet Valley, which is part of the extensive military training area in frequent use.

Our last points of call in Roxburghshire are Morebattle and Linton.

Morebattle is not named after a fight, but was originally Merebotle, the town by the lake. The water in question was Lynton Loch, which extended over 1,000 acres before it was drained in 1832. The parish church, built in the mid-eighteenth century, stands on the site of an older building which was part of the estates of Glasgow Cathedral.

Linton today is a quiet place, but it was not always so. Not only was it the scene of numerous Border raids, but it had a resident monster. The Linton Worm was a dragon which lived in a cave on the north-east slope of Linton Hill near Greenlees Farm on today's maps. It terrorised the neighbourhood in the twelfth century, eating cattle and sheep and driving people from their homes with its scorching breath. At length a brave knight, Somerville of Lariston, resolved to slay the beast. He noticed that the Worm always held its mouth gaping open, so he hit on the idea of putting a large lump of peat, soaked in hot pitch, on his lance and thrusting it down the creature's throat. The plan worked — the Worm choked on the hot peat and suffocated. You can see the dents its great coils made on Wormiston Hill today. Who is to say there is no truth in legends such as these?

Linton Church is also notable in its own way, for it is built on a hillock of pure sand, with no apparent solid foundations. Above the entrance is an ancient panel depicting the slaying of the Worm. From the church, a 4-mile walk leads along the minor road to Bankhead and up on to Linton Hill, returning the same way. Do please ask permission to go on the hill when you reach the farm — you are most unlikely to be refused. You are also most unlikely to find any dragons on Linton Hill today, and can enjoy in peace the splendid views, east to the Cheviot Hills and north into Berwickshire, the subject of the next chapter.

7 Berwickshire

Berwickshire is in shape a squiggly rectangle, with the county town of Duns set right in the middle. We start our exploration of the county on its west side, travelling up the Leader Water through the village of Earlston to the royal and ancient burgh of Lauder. Despite its small size, with a population of under 1,000, Lauder is the only royal burgh in Berwickshire, having held its charter since at least the fourteenth century.

Entering the town from the south, the Tolbooth faces you in the main street. As the name indicates, its original purpose was the collection of tolls from people passing through. The ground floor was used as a gaol for many years. Names around Lauder such as Witches Knowe and Ducking Pool indicate the crimes of which some of those imprisoned here were accused. The upper floor was the Council Chamber, with a platform at the top of the stair from which proclamations could be made. There was previously a market cross in front of the building and a 'tron', an old weighing device for gauging the weight of goods for sale or toll purposes.

The parish church, on the south side of Market Place, is built on the plan of a Greek cross and has an octagonal bell-tower. It was designed by Sir William Bruce, architect to the King, in the 1670s.

Just to the east of Lauder is Thirlestane Castle, an outstanding example of a Border fortress and well worth a visit. It was in fact originally constructed as a

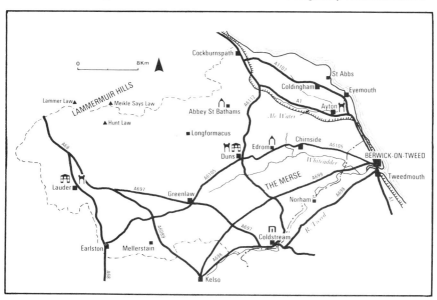

fort but in the sixteenth century was converted into a dwelling-house. It is an imposing red sandstone building with turrets, towers, balconies, and a splendid collection of furniture and paintings assembled by the Earls of Lauderdale over the years. The castle is open to view in the summer months.

Another unusual attraction in Lauder is the Border Country Life Museum, opened in 1982. Displays of photographs, old maps, farm machinery and furniture show the development of social and agricultural life in the region. The Museum, which is attached to Thirlestane Castle, is open from May to September, and there is a combined admission charge for both places.

Lauder has its own Common Riding, held in early August. The riding fell out of custom in the nineteenth century, but was revived to mark the coronation of George V in 1910 and has been held ever since. The full festival lasts a week, with various short rideouts and other events

taking place, but the main activity is on a Saturday. The Cornet takes the burgh flag from the Tolbooth to the Watering Stane, where the Lauderdale foxhounds join the procession. The riders move on to the Burgess Stone, the only boundary marker still standing, and the Cornet adds a stone to the cairn before leading the procession back to the town. In the afternoon there are sports and a gymkhana.

There are splendid walks all round Lauder, and study of the map will reveal numerous tracks leading off the main road which can be used to gain access to the hills on either side. A 5-mile walk leads up the Harry Burn just north of Lauder, heading west to Whitlaw and up on to Inchkeith Hill, and returning on a different track to Trabrown.

A longer walk making a really fine day out starts from the Carfraemill Hotel, at the junction of A68 and A697 about four miles north of Lauder. Take the minor road running due north alongside the Kelphope Burn, diverting on to a track after about half a mile to avoid some of the road walking. Rejoin the road and take the right fork through Tollishill for the track on to Crib Law, at 1,680ft (509m) a splendid viewpoint for the Lammermuir Hills and north to Edinburgh and the Firth of Forth.

You can either return the same way (round trip 11 miles) or extend the walk by striding out along the ridge eastwards for 2 miles to Seenes Law, returning down the lovely valley of the Whalplaw Burn to Longcroft and the main road at Cleekhimin ½ a mile south of Carfraemill (round trip 14 miles).

We shall come back to Edinburgh, but for the moment let us turn east from Lauder. Before heading for Duns a diversion south-east on A6089 leads to Greenknowe Tower and Gordon. The tower, ½ a mile north of the town, was

---

PLACES TO VISIT AROUND LAUDER

Tolbooth, Lauder
Former toll house, also used as a gaol.

Thirlestane Castle
Border fortress. Collection of paintings and furniture, Border Country Life Museum.

Greenknowe Tower
Built in 1581, held by Seton family for many years.

Mellerstain House
Georgian mansion, fine gardens, superb collection of paintings, Adam ceilings.

Mellerstain House and grounds

built in 1581 on the site of an earlier building founded by the knight Aidan de Gordun. In the fifteenth century the line passed to the Seton family, whose coat of arms is carved over the door of the tower.

Gordon is a pleasant small town, having links with the clan of the same name, which settled here before spreading its influence to the Highlands. Three miles south of Gordon, west of the main road, is Mellerstain House, one of Scotland's finest Georgian mansions. It was built in the 1720s by William and Robert Adam for the Baillie family. The gardens were laid out in 1909 by Sir Reginald Blomfield and include many fine trees, avenues and a lake. Mellerstain is now the home of Lord and Lady Binning and the house, which contains a superb collection of paintings, including works by Van Dyck, Constable and Gainsborough, and magnificent Adam ceilings, is open over Easter and from May to the end of September. There is a gift shop and tea room.

From Mellerstain a minor road leads east to Hume, passing Hume Castle, a good example of the early design of Border fortified houses, featuring a square enclosure or quadrangle with a tower at each corner. From Hume it is a short run north on B6364 to Greenlaw, which preceded Duns as the county town. The town contains a number of fine buildings, perhaps notably the imposing Town Hall, built in 1830, and the Castle Hotel from a year later. The church was built in 1675 and restored in the nineteenth century. The tower, which appears to be part of the church, is in fact separate from it and was used as a prison. There is trout fishing on the Blackadder from March to early October; permits from the post office or hotels in Greenlaw.

The A6105 road from Greenlaw to Duns passes two places of interest. Off the road to the south is Marchmont House, another Adam building from that fruitful period in the mid-eighteenth century. The house is now the home of Sir Robert and Lady McEwen and the gardens are open in the summer months. A little further on is the village of Polwarth, a place of rural quiet but with a curious and appealing custom from the past. Whenever a marriage was cel-

ebrated in the village, all the villagers would dance round the two old thorn trees on the green. The trees are still there although the dancing has long since ceased.

Duns was the county town of Berwickshire from 1903 until local government reorganisation in 1975 made it, instead, the administrative centre for Berwickshire District Council. The name derives from an old word for a hill fort, and the original settlement was on the slopes of Duns Law. Here in 1639 two armies — those of the English King, Charles I, and the Scottish Covenanters under General Sir Alexander Leslie — opposed each other for a period of three weeks, without battle being joined. A treaty was then signed and the armies withdrew — a rare example of a bloodless encounter in Border history. The block of sandstone atop Duns Law is still known as the Covenanters' Stone; it was enclosed in 1878 because souvenir hunters were chipping too much of it away!

In Newtown Street, together with the council offices, you will find the Jim Clark Memorial Room, a rather unusual type of museum. It commemorates the life and career of the racing driver who lived in Duns and was world champion in 1963 and again in 1965. He was killed in a crash in 1968, and the Memorial Room contains many of his trophies, with other mementos of his career, donated by his parents. It is open from Easter to October, every day.

Murray Street, on the other side of the square, leads to the public park, where you can play bowls, tennis, and putting. (For the golfer there is a 9-hole course on the outskirts of the town.) In the park, too, is a bronze statue of John Duns Scotus, scholar and theologian of the late thirteenth and early fourteenth century. It was presented to Duns by the

Jim Clark museum, Duns

Franciscan Order on the 700th anniversary of his birth in 1966. The Latin inscription states that 'Scotland was his cradle, the World his fame, the Rhine his grave, Heaven his soul. Here breathes the spirit of a great man'.

PLACES TO VISIT AROUND DUNS

Jim Clark Memorial Room, Duns
Mementoes of life and career of former world champion motor racing driver.

Duns Castle
Nature reserve, walks, pond with waterbirds.

Marchmont House
Adam building, mid-eighteenth century. Gardens open in summer.

Manderston House
Fine Edwardian country house, well-preserved domestic quarters, stables, park with lake and walks.

Edrom Church
Contains a fine Norman doorway.

Ayton Castle
Red sandstone building, fine decorations and furniture, painted ceilings.

Bunkle Castle
Ruin of Border tower with many historical associations.

Abbey St Bathans
Beautiful village with priory ruins.

Edin's Hall Broch
Fortified structure from first century AD.

Another son of Duns to achieve famewas Sir Joseph Paxton, who started his career as a gardener with the Duke of Devonshire at Chatsworth, in Derbyshire. He began to design buildings for horticultural purposes and went on to design the (original) famous Crystal Palace in London, and many fine fountains. His books *Paxton's Flower Garden* and the *Pocket Botanical Dictionary* were best-sellers in their day.

Paxton would undoubtedly have approved of the creation of a nature reserve in the grounds of Duns Castle, just north of the town. The castle itself, the seat of the Hay family, is strictly private, but the reserve can be visited if you obtain a permit from the warden, Mr W. Waddell, The Mount, Duns. From the car park on B6365 at the north end of the reserve a nature trail leads round the reserve to the 'Hen Poo', a beautiful stretch of water providing an ideal habitat for many types of waterfowl. In the woods you may see woodpeckers, pied flycatchers, and redstarts, and mammals frequenting the reserve include roe deer, red squirrels and badgers.

Duns gives us the last of our twelve Border festivals. It takes place during the first full week in July, starting on a Sunday with the Kirking of the principals (the Duns Reiver and his Lass and the Wynsome Maid o'Duns — all three are chosen by public election). On Monday evening the Reiver takes charge of the burgh flag and rides it round the town to display it to the populace. Tuesday evening's ride goes to the top of Duns Law, where a service is held, and then to the Bruntons, the 'burnt town' where the original buildings of Duns stood before the place was devastated in 1558. On Wednesday afternoon the Maid is crowned in the public park and children's sports are held; that evening

Manderston Gardens, near Duns

the Reiver leads his followers over Duns Common to Harelaw Crags, where a symbolic piece of turf is cut. On Thursday the ride visits Longformacus and there is a firework display, and on Friday the married men do battle with the bachelors at handba'. Those with energy left attend the Reivers Ball. On the Saturday the festival ends with the riding of the parish bounds, sports and a fancy dress parade before the flag is returned by the Reiver to the President of the Duns Festival Committee for safe keeping until the next year.

A mile or so east of Duns is Manderston, one of the finest Edwardian country houses in Britain. A feature of particular interest is the 'downstairs' — the domestic quarters which are preserved to give a real insight into life in such a house eighty to ninety years ago. The stables too are splendidly preserved. In the house itself are magnificently decorated staterooms, a 'silver staircase' and fine furniture and hangings. The 56-acre park with its lake has formal and woodland gardens with walks laid out. Manderston, the home of Mr and Mrs

Adrian Palmer, is open on Sundays and Thursdays through the summer, and on Bank Holiday Mondays.

Further along A105 is Edrom, where the church contains a fine Norman doorway. It is the only remnant of the original building, dating from about 1140; the church was rebuilt in 1732. In the manor house, a school for cellists has been established, with pupils coming from many overseas countries to study here. At The Dun is Edrom Riding Centre, where horses can be hired for an hour or longer according to your wishes.

The next village eastwards is Chirnside, a T-shaped settlement with a long street running along the hill slope. The church is the oldest building in the village by some way; as with Edrom, a Norman doorway, at the west end, survives. At the east end of the village, a prehistoric grave was excavated in 1906 and was found to be that of a chieftain of the Beaker Folk. A cairn marks the site today. A plant in Chirnside makes the paper covers for the tea bags we use so often.

Four more miles eastwards on B6355 from Chirnside brings us to the pleasant village of Ayton, on the A1 and near to the Eye Water, on which trout fishing is available in season. Ayton has two interesting churches and a castle. The Old Church dates back to the twelfth century and bears an unusual dedication, to St Dionysius. It was the site of several meetings in the fourteenth and fifteenth century between Scottish and English parties to discuss truce and border-line arrangements. The church, now largely in ruins, lies to the east of the present parish church, built in 1864 on the Gothic style. The spire is 130ft high.

Ayton Castle is an imposing building of red sandstone, designed by James Gillespie Graham, who was also responsible for Brodick Castle on the Isle of Arran, which is markedly similar to Ayton. The castle was built for William Mitchell-Innes, who was at the time Governor of the Bank of Scotland. It has been a family home ever since, except for a period in World War II when it was used as a school. The castle is open to view on Wednesdays and Sundays in the summer months; the entrance hall, dining room and library all contain very fine Victorian decoration and furniture, with splendid painted ceilings.

Leaving the coast to the next chapter, **we turn north along the A1**, following the Eye Water and the main east coast rail line and passing through Reston, where a fortnightly auction market is held throughout the year. Instead of continuing north, an interesting diversion can be made by turning left here, westwards along the northern edge of the Merse, the area of rich Berwickshire farmland between the coast and the hills. The B6438 leads through the scattered parish of Bonkyl or Bunkle, with several ruined castles of which Bunkle itself, $\frac{1}{2}$ a mile west of Marygold village, is perhaps the best preserved. The name is thought to mean 'the place of the cell' and there has been a parish church since at least 1420. The present church, at Preston, is fairly recent, having been built in 1820.

Three miles west from Preston on B6355, a right turn on to a minor road leads to Abbey St Bathans in the valley of the Whiteadder Water. Before reaching the river, you pass, on the north-east slopes of Cockburn Law, the impressive Edin's Hall Broch, one of only ten such structures in the whole of Lowland Scotland. The broch, which is open to view at any time, measures 90ft in diameter and the walls, which contain small rooms or cells, are up to 19ft thick.

Chirnside Church

Around the broch are double earth ramparts; this was a significant fortress when it was occupied — probably in the first and second centuries AD.

A good way of seeing the broch is to follow the walk from Abbey St Bathans waymarked by the regional council. The walk leaves the village heading east along the road; where the road meets the river, it crosses by the footbridge and climbs steeply through the wood (this valley contains almost a third of the oak woodland in the Borders Region and is an important habitat for birds and wild flowers). Follow the track, now heading away from the river, for a mile to the road, where you turn right for another mile to Elba Wood. The name does not come from the island in the Mediterranean but possibly from Gaelic words meaning a hill dwelling.

Turn right off the road and take the forest track to the river, crossing it by a footbridge near Elba Cottage. There was once a copper mine in this area, but it was abandoned in the 1820s. The walk continues on the south side of the river, gradually climbing on to Cockburn Law and the Broch. The return to Abbey St Bathans is made by walking north-west to the sharp bend in the road known locally as 'Toot Corner' — very apt!

There was a priory of Cistercian nuns in Abbey St Bathans in the late twelfth century. The priory was badly damaged during English raids in the sixteenth century but the east gable and north wall are still there, incorporated into the present church. The name itself is something of a mystery as it seems certain that the priory never attained abbey status. The gardens of Abbey House are sometimes open to the public — enquire locally.

Leave this peaceful spot the way you came in and turn right on B6355 to take another small back road leftwards where the road meets the Whiteadder at Ellem, to the hill village of Longformacus. The village contains a church with a long history — originally dedicated in 1240, it was rebuilt in 1710 and restored in the 1890s. It is also an excellent centre for walks on the Lammermuir Hills. West from the village, a track leaves the road after $\frac{1}{2}$ a mile and passes through Whinrig to Watch Water Reservoir, set in a valley amid fine hill scenery. The round trip is about five miles. It could be extended by turning north from the reservoir to the Dye Water valley and regaining the road via Horseupcleugh, a distance of about nine miles, or eleven if you walk back along the road to Long-formacus.

Two more hill walks will give the flavour of the Lammermuirs — a wide stretch of pretty empty country, but very satisfying walking terrain and with generally excellent views, northwards to Edinburgh and the Firth of Forth and eastwards to the sea. The first walk is circular, of about nine miles, and starts from St Agnes, just in Lothian Region on the B6355. Walk north along the track that follows the Bothwell Water up into the hills, to the farmstead of Belton Dodd. Turn north-west here, between the Mossy Burn and West Burn, and in about a mile, turn west on a cross-track that crosses the valley of the West Burn and climbs on to Spartleton Edge. The return route follows this fine ridge all the way back to the starting point, keeping to the higher ground and thus enjoying the best of the views. This outing should take no more than five hours; it is generally quite easy walking, though the navigation in the centre section would need a little care in poor visibility.

The second walk traverses the southern part of the Lammermuirs, and is linear, so transport would have to be arranged at either end. It starts from

Pyatshaw, on the A697 about three miles east of Lauder. Take the minor road running up the east bank of the Brunta Burn and cross the burn after $\frac{1}{2}$ a mile on the track leading to Blythe. Just past Blythe, take the right fork and follow this path in a north-easterly direction, keeping to the higher ground over Nun Rig and crossing Blythe Edge to drop into the valley of the Dye Water at Byrecleugh.

Turn more north-westerly here to climb up to the Mutiny Stones and Long Cairn, an earthwork about 60 yards in length and a good place for a break.

Your way from here is north, then north-east at a fork to pass Killpallet before reaching the road at Duddy Bank. This is a total distance of about ten miles; an energetic walker could extend the day by another 2 miles, continuing on the track west of Faseny Water through Penshiel to meet the 'support party' at the west end of Whiteadder Reservoir, a pleasant place for them to wait.

Having glimpsed the coast on these walks, it is now time to consider its attractions in more detail.

8 The Coast

The high and rugged coast of Berwickshire

The coastline covered in this chapter is all in Berwickshire, but it has such character, and that character is so different from the rest of the Borders, that it fully deserves to have a chapter to itself. Coastal areas are always fascinating; the interplay between land and sea, constantly changing as the tide makes its restless pilgrimages, is a delight to the eye. The birdlife is plentiful and varied, and all the small settlements are packed with their own distinctive character and with history.

The Berwickshire coast is rocky, dramatic in outline, and served by very few roads. It is not a place for the idling holidaymaker looking for a wide beach with at his back the full facilities of a resort. It is still a working coast, as we shall see, with a fishing fleet. Above all, it is a coast rarely visited and well worth exploring. Take a few days and work your way north along it before plunging into the heady whirl of Edinburgh. You won't regret it.

The first settlement on the Scottish side — north, that is, of the piece of Scotland stolen by the English 500 years ago — is Lamberton, a tiny place on the landward side of the present A1. Its main claim to fame is that its church was the scene of the betrothal vow of James IV of Scotland and Margaret Tudor in 1503; the ruins of the church can be seen, but Habchester Fort, up on Lamberton Moor, is in private hands and cannot be viewed close to.

The first truly coastal settlement is Burnmouth, 3 miles north of Lamberton. Driving along the A1, or passing by in a train, you would not know there was a settlement here at all — it is so well hidden down its steep ravine. Nonetheless, there it is and it still remains active in lobster and crab fishing. It has seen its moments of history, despite its small size; being the first place in Scotland on the coast. Burnmouth was the scene of the signing of two of the many treaties between England and Scotland, in 1384 and 1497. It would not be chosen for events of such importance today!

Two miles north of Burnmouth, the Eye runs into the North Sea, forming as it does a natural harbour round which the town of Eyemouth has grown up. The first fishermen to exploit this facility are believed to have been Benedictine monks from Coldingham Priory, in the thirteenth century. Eyemouth became a burgh in 1597 and was granted the status of a free port. From then until the late nineteenth century, haddock and herring fishing flourished with a fleet of upwards of thirty vessels. On 14 October 1881 there occurred here one of those terrible tragedies that seem to visit fishing communities everywhere.

A fleet of thirty vessels had gone out from Eyemouth, along with ships from other ports. A great storm blew up and the fleet turned for home. They were caught, and only a few of the ships managed to make the run into harbour without the sea tearing them apart or hurling them onto the rocks. Of the awful total of 191 men drowned that day, 129 were from Eyemouth. The town was left with over 100 widows and 350 children without fathers.

The centenary of the disaster was marked by various events in 1981, among them the opening of a fine new museum in the former Auld Kirk. The Tourist Information Centre is in the same building. The museum tells the story of the 1881 storm and there are other exhibits showing how fishing has

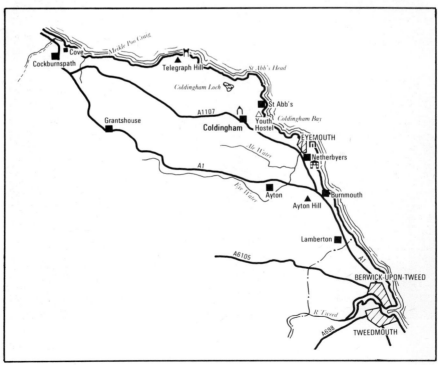

Eyemouth harbour

PLACES TO VISIT ON THE COAST

Eyemouth Harbour
Fishing vessels, smoking houses, bathing, walks.

Eyemouth Museum
Story of the disaster of 1881, development of fishing, tapestry of disaster.

Netherbyres
Eighteenth-century house outside Eyemouth. Gardens open in summer.

Coldingham Priory
Founded 1098, still used for public worship.

St Abb's Head
Nature reserve, many seabirds breeding, walks, fine cliff scenery.

Fast Castle
Extraordinary ruin perched on a 'stack' — access difficult but worthwhile!

---

changed over the centuries and how the town itself has developed. A notable exhibit is a 15ft long tapestry depicting the 1881 disaster. It was sewn by local women, all of them descendants of men who were drowned that day, and it contains one million stitches. A labour of love indeed. The museum is also the start of Eyemouth Town Trail which links eight story-boards around the town a⌐ ⌐rbour.

⌐outh harbour is still a busy
⌐ all the fascination of any port
⌐ are active. Fishing these
· for white fish, prawns,
⌐. You can see fish being
⌐ned, and if you are

lucky, being filleted and smoked in traditional smokehouses. There is a boat building and repair yard across the harbour. The Eyemouth fishermen are not, legally, permitted to fish for salmon, as the seas outside the harbour limits are in legal terms considered as being part of the River Tweed. It makes little logical sense, but that is the way of it.

Eyemouth has a surprising range of facilities for the sportsman. Sea angling is well established, with a thriving local club, and boats can be hired to fish for cod, mackerel, flounder, sole and haddock. There is coarse fishing on the Eye Water inland from the town. Eyemouth has a 9-hole golf course, the only one on this stretch of coast. There is safe sea bathing and a modern indoor swimming pool. Sailing is growing in popularity. Bowls and tennis are available in season.

Well worth a visit are the gardens of Netherbyres, an eighteenth-century house just south of the town. The gardens are oval in shape and are walled; they are open in the summer months.

There is a splendid 4-mile coast walk from Eyemouth up to Coldingham and St Abbs, the next two villages northwards. The walk is waymarked and follows the cliff-top most of the way. At Coldingham Bay you can either turn left into the village or walk on for an extra $\frac{1}{2}$-mile or so to St Abbs. There is a bus service between Coldingham and Eyemouth, or for a longer day the walk could simple be reversed — coastal scenery is always worth studying in both directions. On this walk you will see a variety of birdlife, coastal plants such as sea pinks, sea bindweed and vipers bugloss, and exposed volcanic rock.

Coldingham village is so well tucked into its sheltered valley, fed by the Buskin Burn, that even from $\frac{1}{2}$ a mile

Coldingham Parish Church, founded 1147

away you would not know there was a settlement there at all. It was granted burgh status in 1638 and was at that time an important religious centre, with the Benedictine priory at its heart. Here were seen royal visitors, state occasions such as the peace conference after Flodden, and at one time a garrison of several thousand militia.

The priory was founded in 1098 by Edgar, King of Scots, thus making it one of the oldest establishments of its kind in Scotland. Edgar's building, dedicated to St Cuthbert, was in fact erected on the site of an even older church, to St Mary. The tower stood 90ft at its full height; alas, like so many fine buildings of the Borders, it suffered repeated damage, notably by Cromwell in 1648. Public worship is still observed at the priory, which is open to visitors all the year

round free of charge.

Coldingham has several hotels, a youth hostel, and facilities for caravans and tents. There is a small studio in the village where art classes are held each summer. Sea angling is available, as are skin-diving and sailing; trout can be fished on Coldingham Loch, 2 miles north. Numerous walks are possible from the village, one of the best leading back through St Abbs to St Abbs Head, a noted bird reserve.

St Abbs takes its name from Ebba, a sister of King Oswy of Northumbria. She founded a religious community here in the seventh century. It is said that when St Cuthbert visited her, he was in the habit of immersing himself in the sea for long periods — not for recreation but as a means of prayer, and the seals, so the story goes, came to him and stayed by his side. You can still bathe with safety, and you are still very likely to see seals, which breed in great numbers on the Farne Islands off the Northumberland coast. I doubt if they will come as close as they are reputed to have done to Cuthbert, but they are far from shy.

The walk from the village to the headland is only about a mile and a half but it is not to be missed. The cliff scenery is among the most dramatic of the whole coast, rising to 310ft at St Abb's Head itself. Bird life abounds, and as well as a lighthouse there are a number of settlement sites dating from prehistoric times. If your time is limited you can drive to the reserve along a lane from Coldingham, to a car park near the headland.

St Abb's Head was purchased by the National Trust for Scotland in 1980 and is managed jointly with the Scottish Wildlife Trust. The reserve covers 192 acres of cliff and coastal area. The rocks here are mainly lavas from volcanoes which were active in the area about 400 million years ago. If you stand at Pettico Wick, at the west end of the reserve, and look north along the coast, you can clearly see the two predominant types of rock — banded and folded sediments on one hand and unstructured solidified lavas on the other.

St Abb's Head is an important breeding area for seabirds, as might be expected. Among the species to be seen here, especially between April and July, are guillemots, razorbills, kittiwakes, fulmars, and sometimes puffins. Land birds on the reserve include wheatears, meadow pipits and stonechats. Kitti-

St Abbs, Berwickshire

wakes can also be seen bathing on the Mire Loch, a pond which was dammed in 1901.

The reserve is open all the year round and the ranger, Stephen Warman, will be pleased to tell you more about it. He can be contacted at Ranger's Cottage, Northfield, St Abbs — groups planning to visit the reserve should always contact him in advance.

Three miles west of St Abb's Head is one of the most extraordinary ruins in all Scotland — Fast Castle, perched almost unbelievably on a stack, not even on the main cliff, and accessible only via a gangway after a cliff-face descent that would test the strongest nerve. You can see the ruin from above, and that may be enough for most people. Even to get so far requires a decent walk — the nearest road is the A1107 2 miles away at Meikle Black Law. A round trip on foot from Coldingham to Fast Castle, using lanes via Lumsdaine and across the Dowlaw Burn, and then back to the road via Dowlaw itself, would cover about six miles and make an unusual and satisfying excursion. You would, of course, need a driver to collect you.

Fast Castle was used by Sir Walter Scott as the model for Wolf's Crag in *The Bride of Lammermuir* — for once there was no exaggeration in the description! It was also used by the fourteen-year-old princess Margaret Tudor as a resting place on her way north to marry James of Scotland. Why stop here? It is a mystery indeed, when the priory at Coldingham would surely have been the logical place. These are things to reflect on as you stand on the cliffs at Fast Castle Head and look out at a sea which itself seems to have a fair appetite for taking ships and men. There have been any number of wrecks along this coast, and they still occur, despite modern navigational aids such as St Abb's lighthouse.

The coast winds on, round headlands and through bays with names that stay in the memory — Black Bull, Meikle Poo Crag, Pease Bay — to the tiny fishing settlement of Cove, with its secluded harbour. Cove is an example of a 'heugh-heid' (clifftop) fishing village. The harbour is too small to hold many houses; so they were built at the top of the cliff, on the nearest bit of flat ground. Cove harbour was built between 1770 and 1831 to designs by Sir John Hall; today it offers a beautiful spot for a bathe or a picnic.

A mile or so inland is Cockburnspath (usually said as Co'path), on the A1 but alas, no longer with a railway station. There is a fine Mercat Cross with a rose and thistle emblem. Co'path is to be the eastern terminus for the Southern Upland Way long distance footpath, which begins its 230-mile journey across Galloway and the Borders at Portpatrick, near Stranraer. I would hope any walker covering the whole path will take the extra mile to reach the coast and thus truly walk sea to sea.

As for us, we are on the busy A1 and within an hour or so's driving distance of Edinburgh. It has beckoned at various points throughout this book, and its call can be resisted no longer.

9 Edinburgh

Inset: Changing the guard at the castle

The centre of Edinburgh looking west

To describe the vast range of attractions in and around Edinburgh in a single chapter is a difficult, if not impossible, task. The best I can do is to summarise some of the many things the visitor can see and do in this fine city and refer to further sources of information. Edinburgh is a city geared to the reception of visitors and you will find no shortage of literature or helpful people.

Scotland's capital city is founded on hills — volcanic plugs, the most dramatic of which, Castle Rock and Arthur's Seat, give the city its unique and splendid skyscape. From anywhere in the city centre or the surroundings you can see these strong outlines rising to dominate the view. At the centre lie the Royal Mile and Princes Street, dividing the Old Town and the New.

Edinburgh was originally named Dunedin — 'fortress on a ridge' — and there is of course another city with this name in New Zealand, whither so many Scots emigrated in the eighteenth and nineteenth centuries. In the seventh century, the castle was re-fortified by the Northumbrian king Edwin, and the town was named after him as Edwinesburg. The modern name happily combines elements of both Celtic and Anglian origin.

As the castle is such a dominant feature in the city centre, and has been so important in its long history, it is right that we should begin our tour there. The oldest surviving building is St Margaret's Chapel, dedicated to the wife of King Malcolm III and built in the late eleventh century. Near to it is Mons Meg, the castle's famous fifteenth century cannon, used for many royal salutes in the past. It is not, however, the gun used daily (except Sundays) for the one o'clock time-check — an unusual signal and one that can be somewhat alarming the first time you hear it!

PLACES OF INTEREST IN EDINBURGH

Arthur's Seat and Castle Rock
Hills of volcanic rock which form the capital's foundation.

THE CASTLE
St Margaret's Chapel
Oldest surviving building dedicated to the wife of King Malcolm III built in the late eleventh century.

Mons Meg
The castle's famous fifteenth-century cannon.

Scottish National War Memorial
On the north side of Crown Square and designed by Sir Robert Lorimer.

United Services Museum
On the west side of Crown Square and was opened in 1933.

The Great Hall
On the south side of Crown Square, built in the early sixteenth century by James IV. Still used for banquets and receptions. Weaponry and armour.

Royal Apartments
On the east side of Crown Square, includes the little room where James VI of Scotland and I of England was born to Mary Queen of Scots.

Crown Room
Contains the Scottish Regalia.

Castle Esplanade
Scene for the Military Tattoo held each year during the Edinburgh Festival.

At the heart of the castle is Crown Square, all four sides of which hold interest. The north side is formed by the Scottish National War Memorial, designed by Sir Robert Lorimer and dedicated in 1927. On the west side is the United Services Museum, opened in 1933. Further military mementoes can be found in the Great Hall on the south side of the square. Built in the early sixteenth century by James IV, it once housed meetings of the Scottish Parliament, and is still used for banquets and receptions for important visitors to Edinburgh. There is a most interesting collection of weaponry and armour.

Finally, on the east side of the square are the Royal Apartments, including the little room where James VI of Scotland and I of England was born to Mary Queen of Scots. The view from its windows is impressive, with the castle rock dropping steeply away and the city of Edinburgh beyond. Nearby is the Crown Room holding the Scottish Regalia — the crown, sceptre, sword of state and others.

The Castle Esplanade is the scene for the Military Tattoo held each year during the Edinburgh Festival — an event known world-wide for which tickets are sold out months in advance. There is a fine view south over the city to the Pentland Hills.

Edinburgh Castle is at the head of the Royal Mile, a truly historic thoroughfare and one about which any number of books have been written. One may summarise its main attractions here, but you could easily spend several days wandering up and down and seeing everything that is to be seen.

On the right-hand side, looking down, on the corner of Castle Wynd North, is a house with a cannonball embedded in the wall. The story that it was fired from the castle during the 1745 rising seems

Inside Gladstone's Land painted chamber

sadly not to be true — it marks the gravitation height of the water supply from Comiston Spring to Castlehill Reservoir, which sits just across the road and, with a capacity of over 1½ million gallons, supplies the buildings of Princes Street and neighbouring areas.

On the same sides as the 'cannonball house' is the Outlook Tower and Camera Obscura. The first camera was installed over 100 years ago, but a more modern instrument replaced it in 1945 and on clear days it throws an image of Edinburgh on to a concave circular table; as it does so a commentary tells the history of some of the places depicted. There is a book and craft shop.

Just below the Tower is Mylne's Court, originally built for the family of John Mylne, mason to Charles II. It was restored by Edinburgh University in

1971, the restoration winning a Saltire Society award, and now houses residential students. Across the road a little lower down is Riddle's Court, where you will note the turret staircase outside the building and, inside, the fine painted ceilings. Nearby, Brodie's Close is named after the man whom Stevenson took as the model for Dr Jekyll and Mr Hyde — he was a town councillor by day and a burglar by night.

We are now in Lawnmarket (once Landmarket) which, as the name implies, was where produce was sold — milk, meat and vegetables could be bought here, and on Wednesdays a linen and wool cloth market was held. On the east side of the Lawnmarket is Gladstone's Land, a six-storey tenement built in 1620 for a merchant and burgess, Thomas Gledstanes. It has been restored

THE ROYAL MILE (1)

Cannonball House
On the corner of Castle Wynd North, the house has a cannonball embedded in the wall.

Outlook Tower
Contains a Camera Obscura installed over 100 years ago. Book and craft shop.

Mylne's Court
Built for the family of John Mylne, mason to Charles II.

Riddle's Court
Turreted staircase outside the building and inside are fine painted ceilings.

Gladstone's Land, Lawnmarket
A six-storey tenement built in 1620 for a merchant and burgess, Thomas Gledstanes.

Lady Stair's Close leading to Lady Stair's House
Named after the widow of the first Earl of Stair. She died in 1731. Contains a fascinating collection of manuscripts and momentoes of Burns, Scott and Stevenson.

George IV Bridge
Completed in 1836.

Heart of Midlothian
Design of cobblestones near the great front door of St Giles. Marks the site of the Tolbooth. Despite its original purpose the Tolbooth achieved notoriety as a prison.

St Giles
St Giles the High Kirk, church of the Knights of Thistle. Dates back to 1120. Spire completed in 1495.

Signet Library
Built in 1815 for the Society of Writers to the Signet.

Parliament Hall
Built in 1639 for the Scots Parliament until the Act of Union in 1707.

Edinburgh City Chambers
Intended to be a business exchange when built in 1761. Now used by the sixty-four members of the City of Edinburgh District Council. In the courtyard is a statue of Alexander taming his horse Bucephalus.

Tron Kirk
Church built in 1637 by order of Charles I. Named after the weighing machine that originally occupied the site.

Museum of Childhood
Large collection of historical toys, dolls, books and games. Founded in 1955.

John Knox's House
Dating from the late fifteenth century. Knox was a great preacher and lived there from 1561 to 1572. Many items connected with him are on display.

Netherbow
Church of Scotland's Art Centre designed in the style of an Edinburgh town house. Opened in 1972. Art gallery, shop, theatre, audio-visual studio, restaurant.

Netherbow Port
One of the six original entrances to Edinburgh. Inside the front gateway is the Netherbow Port Bell of 1621.

John Knox's House, High Street

as a typical home of the period, an added attraction being the seventeenth-century shop boots on the Lawnmarket. Gladstone's Land was one of the first properties to come into the care of the National Trust for Scotland in 1934.

Next down from Gladstone's Land is Lady Stair's Close, leading to Lady Stair's House, named after the widow of the first Earl of Stair. She died in 1731.

THE ROYAL MILE (2)

Canongate
Street of fine architectural and historical interest. Note particularly, Chessel's Court, Moray House, Huntly House, and Acheson House.

Canongate Tolbooth
Built in 1591. Recognised by its turreted steeple and large clock. Now a museum of Highland dress and other exhibits.

Canongate Church
Dating from 1688.

Holyrood Brewery
Beer has been brewed here for over 800 years, firstly by the monks of Holyrood Abbey.

Holyrood Palace
Official residence of the Queen when she visits Edinburgh. Earliest parts of the building date from 1530. Many of the state rooms open to view.

Holyrood Abbey
On the south side of the palace, founded in 1128.

Holyrood Park
Contains the Palace and is a magnificent piece of open country.

The house belongs to the District Council and contains a fascinating collection of manuscripts and mementoes of three giants of Scottish literature — Burns, Scott and Stevenson.

Crossing the road to the west side, cross also George IV Bridge, completed in 1836. On the street corner are three brass plates set in the road, marking the site of the last public execution held in Edinburgh, when a murderer, George Bryce, was hanged here in 1864. Passing the statue of the 5th Duke of Buccleuch, you find, near the great front door of St Giles' Cathedral, the 'heart of Midlothian' — a design of cobblestones which marks the site of the Tolbooth. Although the Tolbooth was built to serve the purpose its name implies, to collect tolls, from 1640 onwards it achieved notoriety as a prison. Heads of victims of the scaffold were displayed on the north face of the building, which was demolished in 1817.

On the east side of the cathedral were the Luckenbooths (locked booths), built in the mid-fifteenth century to sell provisions and goods to the people of Edinburgh. They, too, fell to the demolishers in the early nineteenth century. The cathedral remains: St Giles, the High Kirk, church of the Knights of the Thistle. The oldest part, four massive pillars, goes back to 1120, but most of the building dates from the fifteenth century, the crown spire being completed in 1495. The Thistle Chapel, with its superb carved interior, was designed by Sir Robert Lorimer and built in 1911.

On the west side of Parliament Square is the Signet Library, built in 1815 for the Society of Writers to the Signet — the Scottish equivalent of solicitors and lawyers. The Upper Hall is a fine piece of interior design. This building was used for the inaugural procession of the Knights of the Thistle in 1911, and their processions still assemble there.

Parliament Hall was used by the Scots Parliament from the time of its completion in 1639 until the Act of Union in 1707. It is a magnificent building with a hammerbeam roof and stained glass windows, still a busy place as it is used by lawyers from the adjoining courts for consultations with their clients and

PRINCES STREET AND THE 'NEW TOWN'

Planned in 1767 following Parliamentary approval for the extension of the city. Designed by James Craig.

Charlotte Square
Finest part of the 'new town' at the west end of George Street.

No 5 Charlotte Square
Headquarters for the National Trust for Scotland. No 7 has been opened as an example of the house of the period.

Royal Scottish Academy of Painting, Sculpture and Architecture
Established 1826. Annual exhibitions run from May to August. Special show for the festival in September.

National Gallery of Scotland
Large and important collection of paintings.

Scott Monument
200ft Gothic Spire, erected in 1844 to the design of George Meikle Kemp. Depicts characters from Scott's books and poems. Monument open all year round and the climb of nearly 300 steps to the top is worth the effort.

Princes Street Gardens
Fine floral displays. Oldest floral clock in the world dating from 1903.

Scottish National Portrait Gallery
Founded 100 years ago. Contains portraits of famous Scots covering the past 400 years. Also National Museum of Antiquities.

New Town Conservation Centre
No 13a Dundas Street. Guided walks from May to September. Pamphlet called *Four Walks in Edinburgh New Town* for sale.

Calton Hill
Several places of interest including, the Nelson Monument, National Monument, and the City Observatory.

Chambers Street
Houses the Royal Scottish Museum, Edinburgh School of Arts and Adam House, the theatre and conference hall for the University.

Royal Botanic Gardens
Fine collection of trees and plants. Covers all aspects of botany and horticulture.

Scottish National Gallery of Modern Art
Modern sculpture from Inverleith House of artists such as Picasso, Moore and Hepworth.

Inverleith Park
Pond, children's playground, tennis courts, bowling greens and walks.

---

colleagues. The Laigh (or low) Hall was used by Oliver Cromwell as a stable. In Parliament Hall is a statue of Sir Walter Scott, who served as advocate and Sheriff of Selkirkshire for many years.

Opposite St Giles are Edinburgh City Chambers, where the sixty-four members of the City of Edinburgh District Council meet to conduct their business, with the Lord Provost in the chair. The building was completed in 1761, but was little used at first; it was

Holyroodhouse Palace

intended to be a business exchange, but the merchants of the time preferred to conduct their business in the street! The Chambers are eleven storeys high, one of the tallest buildings on the Royal Mile. In the courtyard is a statue of Alexander taming his horse Bucephalus, and within the arches facing the street are

church was built in 1637 by order of Charles I, to house the congregation displaced from St Giles when the latter became a cathedral. The Tron Kirk was closed for worship in 1952, but it is hoped that the interior will eventually become a heritage and information centre for the city of Edinburgh.

Continuing down the west side of High Street, and crossing Blackfriars Street, you come to the Museum of Childhood, in Hyndford's Close. It has a large collection of historical toys, dolls, books and other items and also covers children's games, education and health. The Museum was founded in 1955.

Opposite the museum is John Knox's House, dating from the late fifteenth century. It displays many interesting features, including its overhanging upper floors and an outside stair added in the sixteenth century. The house was saved from demolition in 1850, when the High Street was to be widened, and was then renovated at considerable expense. Knox, the great preacher, lived here from 1561 to 1572 and many items connected with him are on display.

Beside Knox's house, and contrasting nicely with it, is the Netherbow, the Church of Scotland's Arts Centre. Designed in the style of an Edinburgh town house, it was opened as recently as 1972. It contains an art gallery, shop, a small theatre, audio-visual studio, and an excellent restaurant. In the street outside, brass plates mark the site of the Netherbow Port, one of the six entrances to the original town of Edinburgh. A bronze model of the Port can be seen above the entrance to the Arts Centre, and inside the front gateway is the Netherbow Port Bell of 1621. The Netherbow was the point of entry for Prince Charlie in the 1745 rising.

High Street has given way to Canongate, originally a separate burgh owned

memorials to the dead of both world wars.

At the crossing of the Royal Mile and the South and North Bridges is the Tron Kirk, named after the weighing machine that stood on the site previously. The

The Scott Monument

by the canons of the Abbey of Holyrood. Much excellent restoration has been carried out here in recent years — note, for instance, Chessel's Court on the south side with its fine arcades.

Moray House, a little lower down, has a long history. It was built in 1628 for Mary Sutton, daughter of Lord Darnley and widow of the first Earl of Home. Charles I visited the house on a number

OTHER ATTRACTIONS AROUND EDINBURGH

LEITH
Port and dockyard for Edinburgh for centuries. Interesting history and architecture.

Leith Walk
4-mile walk of special interest through the city.

Saughton Rose Garden, Balgreen Road
Scented garden primarily developed for the enjoyment of blind people.

Lauriston Castle
Commenced in the sixteenth century by Sir Archibald Napier, father of John, the inventor of Logarithms. Fine furniture, tapestries and china. Open daily except Friday. Croquet lawns.

Corstorphine Hill
Pleasant wooded area leading to Edinburgh Zoo. Open all year. Covers 80 acres. Comprehensive collection of various species.

Ingliston Showground
Site of the Royal Highland Show each June. Also regular motor racing events.

The Braidwood and Rushbrook Fire Museum, McDonald Road
Contains uniforms, equipment and machinery associated with the fire service. Visits by prior arrangement. Tel: 031 229 7222.

Shrubhill Works, Leith Walk
Transport museum. Open every day except Sunday. Free admission.

of occasions, and Oliver Cromwell made his Scottish headquarters here in 1648. In May 1650 a party of notable people visiting Edinburgh for the marriage of Lady Mary Stuart to Lord Lorne took the opportunity to watch from the balcony the cart carrying the Marquis of Montrose passing on its way to Parliament House, where he was sentenced to death. In 1707, signatures were appended to the Treaty of Union in the gardens of Moray House. It is now a teacher training college.

On either side of Bakehouse Close, a property once owned by the Incorporated Bakers of Canongate, stand Huntly House and Acheson House. Huntly House, built in 1570, shows the projecting upper floors with plastered timber that were common in such buildings. On the exterior are four plaques which are said to answer criticism aroused by the building's fine architecture. One says 'As thou art master of thy tongue so am I master of my ears'. Huntly House was restored in 1932 and is now a museum of local history. Among the exhibits are a copy of the 1638 National Covenant and mementoes of the life of Field Marshal Earl Haig.

Acheson House is a little later in origin than Huntly House, dating from the 1630s. It was built for Sir Archibald Acheson, later a Baronet of Nova Scotia and Secretary of State for Scotland. It was restored by Robert Hurd in 1937 and is now the headquarters of the Scottish Craft Centre. Craftwork from all parts of Scotland can be seen on display and purchased here.

Across the street is the famous Canongate Tolbooth, easily recognised by its large clock and turreted steeple. Built in 1591, it served as the council house and jail for the burgh of Canongate. The clock dates from 1820 and replaced an

Central Edinburgh looking east

earlier model. The Tolbooth is now a museum with a collection of Highland dress and other interesting exhibits.

Next to the Tolbooth is Canongate Church, dating from 1688. Prisoners captured by the Stuart army in 1745 at the battle of Prestonpans were housed here. Notable people buried in the kirkyard include the economist Adam Smith, author of *The Wealth of Nations;* Mrs Maclehose, the original of Robert Burns' 'Clarinda'; and the poet Robert Fergusson, whose headstone was paid for by Burns.

We are now approaching the foot of the Royal Mile, with the gates of Holyrood Palace in front of us. On the right, before crossing Horse Wynd (which once led to the Royal stables) is the Holyrood Brewery. Beer has been brewed here for over 800 years, firstly by the monks of Holyrood Abbey and later by the Younger family. The large brewery on the site today is owned by Scottish and Newcastle Breweries.

Holyrood Palace is the official residence of the Queen when she visits Edinburgh. The earliest parts date from 1530, but most of the building you see today was built by Robert Mylne, the King's Mason, for Charles II in 1671-6. Many of the state rooms are open to view when the Royal Family are not in residence. The picture gallery has no less than 111 portraits of Scottish monarchs by the Dutch painter Jacob de Wit, working on the orders of Charles II. In this gallery, Prince Charlie held dances and assemblies during his occupation of Edinburgh in 1745. It is still used for the annual banquet of the Lord High Commissioner to the General Assembly of the Church of Scotland.

Perhaps the two finest rooms are the throne room, used for investitures, and the dining room, with its green and white Adam-style decorations. The State apartments contain French and Flemish tapestries and fine eighteenth-century furniture. When the Palace is open to view, guided tours take place at regular intervals. There is a tea room in Abbey Strand.

On the south-east side of the Palace, and predating it, are the ruins of Holyrood Abbey. It was founded in 1128 after King David I was charged by a stag while on a hunting trip in the area — then a forest. The king tried to grasp the stag's antlers but found himself holding a crucifix set between its horns. The crucifix stayed in his hand while the stag returned to the spring from where it had come. That night, in a dream, the king was bidden to make a House for Canons devoted to the Cross, and the Abbey of the Holy Rood (or cross) was founded as a result.

The Abbey was badly damaged in the revolution of 1688. A new roof put up in 1758 was, unfortunately, incorrectly planned and collapsed not long afterwards. The Abbey has changed little in appearance since that time.

Holyrood Park, which contains the Palace, is a magnificent piece of open country to find in the heart of a city. It rises to 822ft at the summit of Arthur's Seat (an extinct volcanic plug), from where there are superb views in all directions, including a wonderful panorama of the city. There are coach tours around the park in summer, but for a more leisurely exploration, the walking is splendid.

On the south side of the park is Duddingston Loch, a bird sanctuary and nature reserve where many varieties of duck and geese can be seen, especially in winter when they congregate here. Duddingston Village has a twelfth-century church with, at its gate, 'jougs', the iron collar and chain once used to punish criminals.

Leaving the old part of Edinburgh for the moment, let us have a look at the 'new town' to the north of the castle, starting with the famous thoroughfare, Princes Street, and its fine gardens. The area between Princes Street and the Castle Rock, now occupied by the railway, was once a loch. The 'new town' was planned in 1767, following Parliamentary approval for the extension of the city. It covers over 100 acres and is now a conservation area subject to strict planning controls.

The area was planned and laid out by James Craig, who was only twenty-three when he won the competition for the design. Perhaps the finest part of the new town is Charlotte Square, at the west end of George Street. The square was designed by Robert Adam in 1791. No 5 Charlotte Square is the headquarters of the National Trust for Scotland and No 7 has been opened by the Trust as an example of a house of the period; the rooms on the lower floors are furnished just as they would have been in the late eighteenth or early nineteenth century. The upper floors serve as the official residence of the Moderator of the Church of Scotland, and No 6, next door, serves in a similar capacity for the Secretary of State for Scotland.

Returning to Princes Street, at the Mound is the Royal Scottish Academy of Painting, Sculpture and Architecture. Established in 1826, it has presented annual exhibitions ever since. Exhibitions run from May to August, followed by a special show for the Festival in September. Nearby is the National Gallery of Scotland. As well as an important collection of painting by Scottish artists, there are many fine works by English and Continental masters stretching from the fourteenth century to Cezanne.

A stroll along the north side of the gardens leads to the Scott Monument, one of Edinburgh's best-known landmarks. It is a Gothic spire 200ft high erected in 1844 to the design of George Meikle Kemp. (A memorial room to Kemp can be seen on the outskirts of Peebles, on the A702 Edinburgh road.) In the niches of the monument are sixty-four statuettes depicting characters from Scott's books and poems. The statue of the writer himself is by Sir John Steell. The monument is open all the year round and the climb up nearly 300 steps to the top may be judged worth the effort for the views it provides. There is no shortage of good refreshment rooms nearby to revive you afterwards!

Princes Street Gardens can occupy a pleasant hour or two. As well as the fine floral displays, there is the oldest floral clock in the world, dating from 1903. Up to 25,000 flower and foliage plants are used in the display on the clock, which is changed several times a year. The hands measure 8ft and 5ft and when filled with plants weigh 80 and 50lb respectively. The quarters are marked by the emergence of a sprightly cuckoo.

Near the clock are two fine war memorials, one to the Royal Scots and the other erected by Americans of Scottish blood. Between the Ross Foundation and the open-air theatre is an eight-ton boulder from Southern Norway, presented in 1978 by the Norwegian Army as a remembrance for the hospitality they received while based in Britain between 1940 and 1945. The open-air theatre stages shows and band performances during the summer and at Festival time, and there are dancing sessions which the visitor is welcome to join.

Walking north from Princes Street along the west side of St Andrew Square, headquarters of banks and insurance firms, and across George Street, leads to

Queen Street and the Scottish National Portrait Gallery, founded just 100 years ago. It contains hundreds of portraits of famous Scots covering the past 400 years. In the same building is the National Museum of Antiquities, portraying the life of Scotland and the Scots from prehistory to the present times.

Down the hill in Dundas Street, at No 13a, is the New Town Conservation Centre, showing the work that has been done and is still going on, to conserve the new town. Guided walks start from here each week from May to September, and a pamphlet called *Four Walks in Edinburgh New Town* is available for sale.

To the east of Princes Street, above Regent Road, is Calton Hill, where there are several places of interest. The Nelson Monument, in the shape of a telescope, was completed in 1816. It is 108ft high and at the top is a time ball which descends each day at one o'clock GMT. The unfinished National Monument was designed as a copy of the Parthenon in Athens. Also here are the City Observatory and monuments to John Playfair, a noted mathematician, and the philosopher Dugald Stewart. In Old Calton Burial Ground is a statue of Abraham Lincoln.

South of High Street are further places of interest. In Forrest Road is Greyfriars Kirk, where the National Covenant was signed in 1638. The graveyard contains ornate tombstones and monuments to once-famous citizens of old Edinburgh. In Candlemaker Row nearby is the statue of the small dog known as Greyfriars Bobby, that stayed by the grave of its master John Grey for fourteen years. Bobby's collar can be seen in Huntly House, Canongate.

Chambers Street houses the Royal Scottish Museum, the Edinburgh School of Arts and Adam House, the theatre and conference hall for Edinburgh University. The Royal Scottish Museum houses collections devoted to archaeology, natural history, geology, technology, and science, with the exhibits ranging from primitive art to space travel. There are frequent lectures and films here.

On the northern edge of the city centre is the Royal Botanic Garden (car parking in Arboretum Road), with a very fine collection of trees and plants including superb shows of rhododendrons in season. The plant houses contain many rare and exotic plants and an exhibition hall covers all aspects of botany and horticulture. The grounds contain an exhibition of modern sculpture from Inverleith House, which presently houses the Scottish National Gallery of Modern Art. Many of the most important modern artists such as Picasso, Moore and Hepworth are represented, with a good selection of Scottish works. This collection is due to be moved in 1984 to the former John Watson's School, which is being converted into an art gallery and museum. Across the road from the Botanic Garden is Inverleith Park, with a pond, children's playground, tennis courts, bowling greens and walks.

Leith Walk runs north-east from the city centre to the docks at Leith. On the way are two unusual attractions. The Braidwood and Rushbrook Fire Museum in McDonald Road contains a collection of uniforms, equipment and machinery associated with the fire service, and can be visited by arrangement with Lothian and Borders Fire Brigade (Tel: 031-229 7222).

Leith Walk itself has, in Shrubhill Works, an interesting transport museum, open every day except Sunday free of charge. There are both full-scale and model exhibits of Edinburgh transport over the centuries.

Leith has served as port and dockyard for Edinburgh for centuries. Cruise ships up to 35,000 tons gross can berth here, and the docks have a busy service running to the North sea oilfields. Old buildings include Trinity House, dating from 1816 and St Mary's Church, Kirkgate, parts of which are fifteenth century. Lamb's House, a merchant's house from the early seventeenth century, was restored in 1958 and is now used as an old people's day centre. It is under the protection of the National Trust for Scotland and can be visited by appointment — contact N.T.S. HQ in Charlotte Square for details.

The original village of Leith began some 800 years ago at the point where the Water of Leith entered the Firth of Forth. Much of the waterway is now a pleasant walk, the 4-mile stretch through the city being especially interesting. The river passes through Dean Village, formerly a centre for grain milling. At one time there were seventy mills on the Water of Leith, and the measure for 1 pint in Scotland was taken as 'three pounds Scots of water from the Water of Leith'. Several of the old buildings in Dean Village have been restored and the riverside walk leads to St Bernard's Well, once a favoured place for drinking mineral waters.

The Water of Leith is taking us westwards out of the city, and further upstream it passes near Saughton Rose Garden (on Balgreen Road), open in the summer months. As well as the marvellous roses there are dahlias, fine herbaceous borders, and a scented garden developed for the enjoyment of blind people.

Off the A90, the road that leads to the Forth Bridge, is Lauriston Castle, commenced in the sixteenth century by Sir Archibald Napier, father of John, the inventor of logarithms. It has been considerably extended, notably by the nineteenth-century banker Thomas Allan. The castle is now owned by the city and contains fine furniture, tapestries, and china. It is open daily except Fridays, and the grounds include croquet lawns.

A walk south-westwards across Corstorphine Hill, a very pleasant wooded area, brings you to Edinburgh Zoo, open all the year and a favourite attraction with children of all ages. The Zoo covers 80 acres and its collection of animals, birds, reptiles and fishes is comprehensive. The largest colony of Antarctic penguins in captivity can be seen here; in the summer months, weather permitting, they take a daily walk from their enclosure — the 'penguin parade'. Mammals of all sizes include all the carnivores — bears, sea-lions and many species of deer, including the rare Pere David's deer.

The Zoo houses a vast range of birds, in the tropical bird house, the parrot garden and in aviaries throughout the park. Ducks, geese and swans are found in their own terraced waterfowl pens. Young people are particularly well catered for at the Children's Zoo — almost a miniature farm, with ponies, calves, lambs, goat kids and lots of farm implements to play with.

Further west still on the A8, near Edinburgh Airport, is Ingliston Showground, where the Royal Highland Show is held over four days each June. The show features livestock of every kind and the recently-completed exhibition hall holds machinery and other static displays. Other exhibitions are held at Ingliston throughout the year, and it also hosts regular motor racing meets for both cars and motor-cycles.

That brings us into the realm of sport, for which Edinburgh is especially well equipped. Permanent facilities include the Commonwealth Pool, at one side of Holyrood Park, and Meadowbank Stadium, at the other. Both were built for the staging of the Commonwealth Games in 1970 (Edinburgh will be hosts again in 1986) and both are open to visitors. As well as the Tartan athletics track, Meadowbank has indoor facilities for up to thirty different sports. A temporary membership scheme is available for visitors to Edinburgh looking for a workout on the squash courts, in the gymnasium, or at the golf driving range.

Another major facility of which Edinburgh is proud is the dry ski slope at Hillend, on the northern slopes of the Pentland Hills. At the time of writing, it claims to be the largest artificial ski slope in Britain; it is open all year and facilities for grass ski-ing are also available. The ski tow and chairlift can be used by walkers to gain quick access to the Pentlands, from where there are splendid views over the city and the Firth of Forth.

Golfers are naturally well provided for; in Scotland's capital it could hardly be otherwise! Golf has been played in the Edinburgh area for at least 500 years and within the city boundary there are over twenty courses. Public courses can be found at Braid Hills, Carick Knowe, Craigentinny, Silverknowes and Porto-bello, and short-hole 'pitch and putt' courses at Inverleith Park.

There are naturally many bowling greens, tennis courts (notably at Craig-lockhart Sports Centre), and putting greens in Edinburgh. Pony treks are organised from the stables at Redford, Colinton. You can ice-skate at the Murrayfield Rink, watch greyhound racing at Powderhall — famous for its professional sprint races, though these are now run at Meadowbank — and enjoy boating and canoeing at Craiglockhart.

THE FESTIVAL

I could not end this brief survey of Edinburgh's attractions without mentioning the world-famous International Festival, held over three weeks in August and early September. The Festival opens with a service in St Giles, attended by the Lord Provost, civic dignitaries, artists and representatives of Scotland's cultural and professional life. The Festival itself includes music, opera, ballet, theatre, modern dance, poetry readings — every aspect of the arts is here. A major film festival is held concurrently with the main event; the military tattoo, already mentioned, is a notable event, and there is also the Fringe.

In recent years the Fringe has been threatening to surpass the main festival in terms of variety and number of events, if not quite in terms of quality. Up to 300 companies, amateur and professional, present shows of every possible kind in every possible setting from theatres, church halls and cinemas to the many open-air performances. Everywhere there seems to be a Fringe event happening; it is an extraordinary kaleidoscope of people and happenings, many of them apparently spontaneous.

Further Information For Visitors _____

BORDERS

TOURIST INFORMATION CENTRES

Coldstream, Henderson Park.
Tel: 2607

Eyemouth, Auld Kirk.
Tel: 50678

Galashiels, Bank Street.
Tel: 55551

Gretna, Annan Road.
Tel: 834

Hawick, Common Haugh.
Tel: 2547

Jedburgh, Murray's Green.
Tel: 3435/3688

Kelso, 66 Woodmarket.
Tel: 23464

Langholm, High Street.
Tel: 581

Melrose, Priorwood Gardens.
Tel: 2555

Moffat, Church Gate.
Tel: 20620

Peebles, High Street.
Tel: 20138

Selkirk, Town Centre.
Tel: 20054

All centres are open for the Easter
weekend and then from May-October,
except for Jedburgh, which is open all
year.

PUBLIC TRANSPORT

The Borders Travel Guide gives
comprehensive timetables for all public
transport services to, from and within
the Scottish Borders. It is available from
the Borders Regional Tourist Board
(address above).

ACCOMMODATION

The holiday guides published by the
Borders Regional Tourist Board and by
Dumfries and Galloway Tourist
Association (addresses above) contain
full lists of hotels and guest houses, self-
catering accommodation, camping and
caravan parks. As a general guide, the
last-named are to be found in the
following towns: Bonchester Bridge,
Cockburnspath, Coldingham, Ettrick
Valley, Eyemouth, Galashiels, Hawick,
Innerleithen, Jedburgh, Kelso, Lauder,
Melrose, Moffat, Peebles, Selkirk, Town
Yetholm, and West Linton.

YOUTH HOSTELS

Broadmeadows
Old Broadmeadows, Yarrowford,
Selkirk TD7 5LZ
Grade 3, 28 beds.
Open: March-end September.

Coldingham
The Mount, Coldingham,
Berwickshire TD14 5PA
Tel: Coldingham 298
Grade 2, 68 beds.
Open: March-end September.

Ferniehurst
Ferniehurst Castle, Jedburgh,
Roxburghshire TD8 6NX
Tel: Jedburgh 3398
Grade 3, 62 beds.
Open: March-end September.

Kirk Yetholm
YH, Kirk Yetholm, near Kelso,
Roxburghshire TD5 8PG
Grade 2, 38 beds.
Open: March-end September.

Melrose
Priorwood, Melrose,
Roxburghshire TD6 9EF
Tel: Melrose 2521
Grade 2, 90 beds.
Open: March-end October; closed
November; open weekends, December-
end February.

Snoot
Roberton, Hawick,
Roxburghshire TD9 7LY
Grade 3, 24 beds.
Open: March-end September.

GOLF

There are 18-hole courses at Galashiels
(Ladhope), Hawick (Vertish Hill),
Kelso, Minto, Moffat, Peebles, and West
Linton. There are 9-hole courses at
Coldstream (The Hirsel), Duns,
Eyemouth, Galashiels (Torwoodlee),
Innerleithen, Jedburgh, Lauder,
Lockerbie, Melrose, Selkirk, and St
Boswells. Full information is given in a
leaflet published by the regional tourist
board.

PONY TREKKING

Bowhill Riding Centre,
Bowhill, Selkirk TD7 5ET
Open: All year.

Bowmont Trekking Centre,
Belford-on-Bowmont,
Yetholm, near Kelso
Open: April-October.

Burnhouse Mains Riding Centre,
Stow, Galashiels
Open: All year.

Cossars Hill Farm Riding Centre,
Ettrick Valley, Selkirk
Open: May-September.

Ferniehirst Mill Lodge,
Jedburgh TD8 6PQ
Open: All year.

Galashiels Riding Centre,
Netherbarn, Galashiels
Open: April-September.

Gamescleuch Riding Centre,
Ettrick Valley, Selkirk
Open: All year.

Glenside Stable,
Cappielaw Road, St Boswells
Open: All year.

Peebles Hydro Riding Centre,
Soonhope Road, Peebles
Open: All year.

Priorwood Pony Trekking Centre,
Priorwood YH, Melrose
Open: April-October.

Snoot YH,
Roberton, Hawick
Open: June-August.

Trail Riders,
The Eagle Hotel, Lauder
Open: April-October.

Whithaugh Park Border Country Estate,
Newcastleton
Open: All year.

A leaflet giving further information is
available from the regional tourist
board.

CYCLING

Cycles can be hired from the following:

J. Byers,
24 Horsemarket,
Kelso

George Pennel Cycles,
3 High Street,
Peebles

Tweed Valley Hotel,
Walkerburn,
Peeblesshire

Daily or weekly hire is available.
Further information can be obtained
from: The Regional Council and from
Spokes (Lothian Cycling Campaign), 30
Frederick Street, Edinburgh EH2 2JR.

CASTLES AND TOWERS

Those buildings listed as AM are
scheduled ancient monuments. The
standard opening times for them are:
April-September, weekdays 9.30am-
7pm, Sundays 2-7pm; October-March,
weekdays 9.30am-4pm, Sundays 2-4pm.

Ayton Castle
Off A1, 5m north of Berwick.
Open: May-September, Wednesday,
Sunday and Bank Holiday Mondays 2-
5pm. Admission charge.
Home of Mitchell-Innes family.

Berwick-on-Tweed
Adjacent to railway station.
Open: All reasonable times. Free.
In ruins.

Bunkle Castle
On B6438, 8m north of Duns
Free. Ruin. AM.

Branxholme Castle
On A7, 4m south-west of Hawick
Private residence, not normally open.

Fast Castle
On coast 10m north-west of Eyemouth
Free. Extraordinary cliff-top ruin,
difficult access. AM.

Floors Castle
Off A6089, 1m north-west of Kelso
Open: Easter weekend and early May-
end September, Tuesday-Friday and
Sunday 11am-4.45pm. Admission
charge.
Home of Duke of Roxburghe. Adam
mansion, fine furniture and paintings,
collection of Victorian birds.

Greenknowe Tower
On A6089, $\frac{1}{2}$m west of Gordon
Free. Turreted tower house. AM.

Hermitage Castle
Off A6399, 16m north-east of Langholm
Admission charge. Towers and walls
intact. AM.

Hume Castle
On B6364, 6m north of Kelso
Open: All year, Monday-Friday 10am-
5pm, Sunday 2-5pm. Admission charge.
Obtain key from Breadalbane Guncraft,
below castle.
Restored in 1794. Hilltop site with fine
views.

Neidpath Castle
On A72, 1m west of Peebles
Open: Easter-mid-October, Monday-
Saturday 10am-1pm and 2-6pm, Sunday
1-6pm. Admission charge.
Fine example of fortified house.

Newark Castle
Off A708, 4m west of Selkirk
Apply to Buccleuch Estates, Bowhill.
Free.

Smailholm Tower
Off B6404, 7m west of Kelso
Free. Outstanding example of sixteenth-
century pele tower, on a rocky knoll.
AM.

Thirlstane Castle
Lauder. Off A68
Open: Mid-May-end September,
Saturday, Sunday, Wednesday,
Thursday, plus national and local
holidays, 12 noon-5pm. Combined
admission charge with Border Country
Life Museum.
Largest of all Border castles. Superb
ceilings, furniture and paintings.

Tinnis Castle
Off B712, 9m south-west of Peebles
(Drumelzier)
Open: All reasonable times. Free. Ruin.

Wark Castle
On B6350, 3m west of Coldstream
Open: All reasonable times. Free. Ruin.

With the troubled history of the
Borders, it is not surprising to find that
there are numerous other ruined towers
and castles on the map. Most of them
are on private land, but some are
mentioned in the text and can be visited.

COMMON RIDINGS AND FESTIVALS

Coldstream Civic Week, early August,
  one week
Duns Reivers Week, mid-July, one week
Galashiels Braw Lads Festival, late June,
  one week
Hawick Common Riding, early June,
  two days
Jethart Callants Festival (Jedburgh), late
  June-early July, two weeks
Kelso Civic Week, mid-July, one week
Langholm Common Riding, late July,
  one day
Lauder Common Riding, early August,
  one day
Melrose Summer Festival, mid-June,
  one week
Peebles March Riding and Beltane
  Festival, mid-June, one week
Selkirk Common Riding, mid-June,
  two days
West Linton Summer Festival, early
  June, one week

Further information and exact dates are
available in a booklet called *Common
Ridings and Festivals,* obtainable from
the regional tourist board.

CRAFTWORKERS

Pictoys
33 High Street, Ayton
Open: Tuesday-Saturday 10am-5pm.
Handmade wooden toys.

Duns Pottery
57 Castle Street, Duns
Open: Daily 9.30am-1pm and 2-5pm.
Full range in earthenware and
stoneware.

The Reiver Gallery
36 Gala Park, Galashiels
Open: Monday-Saturday 9.30am-
5.30pm (closed Wednesday afternoons).
Wide range of Scottish crafts.

Heather Ross Prints
Unit 11, Tweedbank Craft Centre,
Galashiels
Open: Monday-Friday 10am-5pm and
some weekends.
Handprinted household textiles.

Coach House Gallery
Main Street, Gordon
Open: Monday-Friday 11am-5.30pm
(half-day Tuesday), weekends 1.30-
5.30pm.
Paintings and craftwork by Border
artists.

Canongate Gallery
8 Burn Wynd, Jedburgh
Open: Monday-Saturday 9am-5pm
(Thursday half-day). Summer Sundays
2-5pm.
Original paintings, craftwork, toys,
prints, framing service.

Kelso Pottery
The Knowes, Kelso
Open: Monday-Saturday 10am-1pm
and 2-5pm.
Hand-thrown stoneware pottery, richly
decorated.

Woodmarket Gallery
36-38 Woodmarket, Kelso
Open: Monday-Saturday 10am-
12.30pm and 1.30-5pm (Wednesday
half-day).
Designer/craftsman in precious metals.

John and Judy Strachan
Jerdonfield, Jedburgh
Open: Monday-Saturday 9am-6pm.
Loom kits and woven items from bags to
rugs.

Pictprint
Little Broadmeadows, Waverley Road,
Melrose
Cut-out and press-out models in full
colour.

Monteviot Woodcraft
Tower Workshop, Harestanes Mill,
Nisbet
Open: Monday-Friday 9am-5pm,
weekends 2-5pm.
Turned articles in local woods — bread
boards, lamp bases, bowls etc.

Oxnam Pottery
Oxnam
Open: Any reasonable time.
Domestic pottery, casseroles, flower
pots, etc.

Peebles Brass Rubbing Centre
Old Parish Church, High Street, Peebles
Open: April-September, Monday-
Saturday 10am-5pm.
All materials and instructions supplied.

Christian Crafts Centre
Main Street, Reston
Open: Any reasonable time.
Silverwork, pokerwork, engraving,
embroidery.

Pentland Ceramics
Teviot View, Roxburgh
Open: Any reasonable time.
Stoneware pottery.

SPORT AND RECREATION

Angling
Information can be obtained from the following sources:

Angling in the Scottish Borders,
published by the Regional Tourist Board.

J. & A. Turnbull,
30 Bank Street, Galashiels TD1 1EN

Berwick and District Angling
  Association,
12 Hillcrest, East Ord,
Berwick-upon-Tweed

Coldstream and District A.A.,
27 Leet Street, Coldstream

Eyemouth Sea Angling Club,
20 Deanhead Drive, Eyemouth

Eye Water Angling Club,
W.S. Gillie,
Market Place, Eyemouth

Galashiels A.A.,
41 Balmoral Avenue, Galashiels

Hawick Angling Club,
Kelvin, Raeson Park, Hawick

Jedforest Angling Club,
42 Howden Road, Jedburgh

Kelso A.A.,
53 Abbotseat, Kelso

Lauderdale A.A.,
Kingarth, 29 Hillside Terrace, Selkirk

Melrose A.A.,
J. Broomfield,
Douglas Road, Melrose

Peeblesshire Trout Fishing Association,
D.G. Fyffe,
39 High Street, Peebles

St Mary's Angling Club,
6 Greenbank Loan, Edinburgh

Selkirk and District A.A.,
40 Raeburn Meadows, Selkirk

Whiteadder A.A.,
St Leonards, Polwarth, Greenlaw

Yetholm A.A.,
per Messrs J. & D.W. Tait,
The Square, Kelso

The address given is that of the Secretary at the time of writing. Information and permits can also be obtained from tackle shops in Berwick-upon-Tweed, Eyemouth, Galashiels, Hawick, Jedburgh, Kelso, Melrose, Peebles, and Selkirk.

Forest Walks

Cardrona Forest
$3\frac{1}{2}$m east of Peebles on B7062
Three waymarked walks, 2, 3, $4\frac{1}{2}$m.

Craik Forest
Borthwick Water picnic place, on minor road leaving B711 at Roberton
Two waymarked walks, $1\frac{1}{2}$, 3m.

Glentress Forest
2m east of Peebles on A72.
Four waymarked walks, 1, $2\frac{1}{2}$, 4, $4\frac{1}{2}$m.
Wayfaring course also available.

GARDENS

Bowhill
Off A708, 1m west of Selkirk
Open: Easter weekend, then Monday,
Wednesday, Saturday and Sunday in
May, June and September 12.30-6pm;
daily except Friday in July and August.
Admission charge. Wheelchairs and
children under 5 free.
Walks, woods and children's play area.

Dawyck
Off B712, 8m south-west of Peebles
Open: Daily 10am-5pm from 1 April-30
September. Free.
Arboretum, heronry and formal garden.

Floors Castle
Off A608, 1m west of Kelso
Open: Daily 10.30-5pm Easter weekend
and 1 May-end September. Admission
charge.
Garden centre and woodland walks.

The Hirsel
Off A697, 2m west of Coldstream
Open: Daily 10am-5pm all year.
Nature trails, spring flowers and visitor
centre.

Kailzie
Off B7062, 3m east of Peebles
Open: Early April-end October 10am-
6pm. Admission charge.
Woodland walks, walled garden,
wildfowl pond and plant centre.

Lothian Estates Woodland Centre
Off A68, 3½m north of Jedburgh
Open: Sunday and Wednesday
afternoons plus holiday Mondays from
Easter-1 July and mid-September-end
October; Monday, Tuesday,
Wednesday, Saturday and Sunday
afternoons from 1 July-mid-September.
Admission charge.
Visitor centre, woodland walks and
pinery.

Manderston
Off A6105, 1½m east of Duns
Open: Sundays and Thursdays, mid-
May-late September 2-5.30pm. Parties
at any time by appointment. Admission
charge.
Formal and woodland gardens, walks
and stables.

Mellerstain
Off A6089, 3m south of Gordon
Open: Daily except Saturday 1.30-
5.30pm, Easter weekend and 1 May-end
September. Admission charge.
Walks and woods with fine views of
Cheviot Hills.

Netherbyres
Eyemouth
For opening times enquire locally.
Eighteenth-century oval walled garden.

Priorwood
Melrose
Open: 1 April-mid-May and end
October-Christmas Eve, Monday-
Friday 10am-1pm, 2-5.30pm, Saturday
10am-5.30pm; mid-May-end October,
Monday-Saturday 10am-6pm, Sunday
1.30-5.30pm. Free (donation box for
NTS).

Traquair
Off B7062, 7m east of Peebles
Open: Easter-end June, 1 September-
end October, 1.30-5.30pm; July and
August, daily 10.30-5.30pm. Admission
charge.
Woodland and riverside walks, walled
garden and craftworkers.

HISTORIC HOUSES

Abbotsford
Off B6360, 2m west of Melrose
Open: Late March-end October, daily
10am-5pm, Sunday 2-5pm. Admission
charge.
Home of Sir Walter Scott.

Ayton Castle
Off A1, Ayton
Open: Mid-May-late September,
Wednesday and Sunday 2-5pm.

Bowhill
Off A708, 1m west of Selkirk
Open: Easter weekend, then Monday,
Wednesday Saturday and Sunday in
May, June and September 12.30-6pm;
daily except Friday in July and August.
Admission charge. Wheelchairs and
children under 5 free.
Home of Dukes of Buccleuch, restored
nineteenth-century kitchen.

Bemersyde
Off B6350, 4m east of Melrose
For opening times enquire locally.
Home of Earl Haig.

Manderston
Off A6105, $1\frac{1}{2}$m east of Duns
Open: Sunday and Thursday, mid-May-
late September 2-5.30pm. Admission
charge.
Edwardian country house, extensive
domestic quarters.

Mellerstain
Off A6089, 3m south of Gordon
Open: Daily except Saturday, Easter
weekend and 1 May-end September
1.30-5.30pm. Admission charge.
Home of Lord Binning, fine Adam
mansion.

Monteviot House
Off A68, $3\frac{1}{2}$m north of Jedburgh
Open: Wednesday only, early May-late
October 1.30-5.30pm. Admission
charge.
See also Lothian Estates Woodland
Centre under *Gardens*.

Traquair
Off B7062, 7m east of Peebles
Open: Daily from Easter-late October
1.30-5.30pm; July and August 10.30-
5.30pm. Admission charge.

MUSEUMS

Border Country Life Museum
Lauder
Open: Saturday, Sunday, Wednesday
and Thursday plus national and local
holidays, mid-May-end September 12
noon-5pm. Joint admission charge with
Thirlestane Castle. Members of Museum
Trust free.

Castle Jail
Jedburgh
Open: 1 April-end October, Monday-
Saturday 10am-12 noon and 1-5pm,
Sundays 1.5pm. Admission charge.

Chambers Institution
Peebles
See Tweeddale Museum.

Coldstream Guards Museum
Coldstream
Open: Early April-end September, daily except Monday 2-5pm. Admission charge.

Eyemouth Museum
Open: April-late October, Monday-Saturday 10am-12.30pm and 2-5.30pm, Sunday 1.30-5.30pm. Closed Wednesday except during July and August. Admission charge.

Innerleithen, Traquair and Glen Museum
Innerleithen
Open: Easter-late October, Wednesday 2-4pm, Saturday 10am-12 noon, and by arrangement. Admission by donation.

Jim Clark Memorial Room
Duns
Open: Early April-end September, Monday-Saturday 10am-6pm, Sundays 2-6pm. Admission charge.

Mary Queen of Scots House
Jedburgh
Open: Summer months, daily, 10am-12 noon and 1-5.30pm (enquire locally for exact dates). Admission charge.

Museum of Old Ironmongery
Selkirk
Open: Monday-Saturday 10am-5pm. Closed Thursday afternoon. Admission by donation.

Scottish Museum of Wool Textiles
Walkerburn
Open: Easter-end October, Monday-Saturday 9.30am-5pm, Sunday 2-5pm. Admission charge.

Selkirk Museum
(in Public Library)
Open: Mid-May-mid-September, Monday, Wednesday and Friday 2-4.30pm; also Tuesday and Thursday in July and August. Free.

Tweeddale Museum
Peebles
(Chambers Institution)
Open: All year, Monday-Friday 9am-7pm (closes Wednesday at 5.30pm). Free.

Wilton Lodge Museum
Hawick
Open: 1 April-end October, Monday-Saturday 10am-5pm, Sunday 2-5pm; 1 November-end March, Monday-Saturday 10am-4pm. Closed Sunday. Admission charge.

NATURE RESERVES

Barefoots Marine Reserve
Eyemouth coastline
Information from: Lawson Wood, Tighnamara, Pocklawslap, Eyemouth TD14 5AX
Tel: Eyemouth 50741

Duns Castle
Off A6112, 1m north of Duns
Scottish Wildlife Reserve/Duns Castle Trust.
Permits and further information from: The Warden, W. Waddell, 26 The Mount, Duns.

St Abb's Head

3m north of Eyemouth
Scottish Wildlife Trust/National Trust
for Scotland.
Open: All year.
Further information from: The Ranger,
Stephen Warman, Ranger's Cottage,
Northfield, St Abb's.
Tel: Coldingham 443

Yetholm Loch

Scottish Wildlife Trust.
Permit only. Further information from:
Scottish Wildlife Trust, 25 Johnston
Terrace, Edinburgh EH1 2NH.
Tel: 031-226 4602

RELIGIOUS HOUSES

The following historic religious houses
are open to view at all reasonable times.
For exact times and admission charges,
enquire locally.

Abbey St Bathans Priory; Coldingham
Priory; Cross Kirk, Peebles; Dryburgh
Abbey; Jedburgh Abbey; Kelso Abbey;
Melrose Abbey; Selkirk Abbey.

Art Centre

2-4 Market Street
Open: Monday-Saturday 10am-5pm;
June-September 10am-6pm.
Works by Scottish artists. Cafe.

Candle Carvery & The Museum Shop

140 High Street
Tel: 031-225-9566
Open: 10am-5.30pm daily.
Candle making.

Canongate Tolbooth

Canongate
Open: Monday-Saturday 10am-5pm;
June-September 10am-6pm.
Former courthouse, dating from 1591.
Collection of Highland dress and other
exhibits. Scottish stone and brass
rubbing centre.

Edinburgh Castle

United Services Museum
Open: Daily 9.30am-6pm, Sunday
11am-6pm.
Great Hall: collection of weapons and
armour.
Crown Room: collection of the Honours
of Scotland including crown of the
Scottish Kings.
Castle Esplanade: site of the Military
Tattoo.
St Margarets Chapel: eleventh century
and oldest occupied building in
Edinburgh.

Edinburgh Wax Museum

142 High Street
Tel: 031-226 4445
Open: Daily.
Portrays Scotland's history; fantasy land
for children.

The Georgian House
7 Charlotte Street
Open: Monday-Saturday 10am-5pm,
Sunday 2-5pm.
National Trust house of Robert Adam
period.

Gladstone's Land
Lawnmarket
Open: Monday-Saturday 10am-5pm,
Sunday 2-5pm. National Trust.
Restored house built 1620, refurbished
in seventeenth-century style.

The Glass Works
14/16 Holyrood Road
Open: Tuesday-Saturday 10am-6pm.

Huntly House
Canongate
Open: Monday-Saturday 10am-5pm;
June-September 10am-6pm.
Local history museum.

John Knox's House
High Street
Open: 10am-5pm. Closed Sunday.
Fifteenth-century house, renovated and
displaying items connected with John
Knox, the sixteenth-century preacher
and Reformer.

Lady Stair House
Lawnmarket
Open: Monday-Saturday 10am-5pm;
June-September 10am-6pm.
Portraits and relics of Robert Burns, Sir
Walter Scott and R.L. Stevenson.

Lauriston Castle
Cramond Road South
Tel: 031-336-2060
Open: Daily, except Friday, 11am-1pm,
2-5pm; November-March, Saturday and
Sunday only 2-4pm.
Late sixteenth-century towerhouse with
nineteenth-century additions. Period
and reproduction furniture, collections
of Derbyshire Blue John Stone, Wool
mosaics etc.

Museum of Childhood
High Street
Open: Monday-Saturday 10am-5pm;
June-September 10am-6pm.
Toys, dolls, children's costumes etc.

National Gallery of Scotland
Mound
Open: 10am-5pm, Sunday 2-5pm.
Works by Continental, English and
Scottish painters.

National Museum of Antiquities of Scotland
Queen Street
Open: 10am-5pm, Sunday 2-5pm.
Portrays life of Scotland and the Scots
from prehistoric times.

The Netherbow
High Street
Church of Scotland's Art Centre.

New Town Conservation Centre
13a Dundas Street
Open: Monday-Friday 9am-1pm, 2-
5pm.
Walks four times weekly, May-
September.
Exhibition of conservation work in
progress.

Outlook Tower Visitor Centre
Lawnmarket
Open: Daily 9.30am-5pm.
Camera obscura, with commentory of
history of places depicted. Book and
craft shop.

Palace of Holyrood house
Canongate
Open: April-October, Monday-Saturday
9.30am-5.15pm, Sunday 11am-4.30pm;
November-March, Monday-Saturday
9.30am-3.45pm.
Official residence of the Queen in
Edinburgh. Guided tours, tearoom in
Abbey Strand. Sometimes the Palace is
closed at short notice for State visits
(usually for two weeks in late May and
three weeks in late June-early July).

Philatelic Bureau Gallery
Head Post Office, Waterloo Place
Open: Monday-Thursday 9am-4.30pm,
Friday 9am-4pm. Closed Saturday and
Sunday.
Display of British postage stamps.

Queensferry Museum
Local History Museum.

Royal Observatory Visitor Centre
Blackford Hill
Open: Monday-Friday 10am-4pm,
Saturday-Sunday 12 noon-5pm.
Largest telescope in Scotland.
Exhibition on astronomy.

**Royal Scottish Academy of Painting,
Sculpture and Architecture**
The Mound
Open: Monday-Saturday 10am-5pm,
Sunday 2-5pm.

Royal Scottish Museum
Chambers Street

St Cecilia's Hall
Cowgate
Russell Collection of Keyboard
instruments.

Scottish Craft Centre
140 Canongate
Open: Monday-Saturday 10am-5.50pm.
Display of Scottish craftwork.

Scottish Experience Visitor Centre
West End, Princes Street
Open: Daily 10am-6.30pm.
Edinburgh's past on a multi vision giant
screen, plus model of Scotland with over
600 places of interest at the touch of a
button.

Scottish National Gallery of Modern Art
Inverleith House, Inverleith Terrace
Open: 10am-5pm except Sunday, 2-5pm
or $\frac{1}{2}$hr before sunset in winter.
Twentieth centure art. Collection due to
move to the former John Watson's
School in 1984.

Scottish National Portrait Gallery
Queen Street
Portraits of famous Scots.

SPORT

Golf
Public courses are at Braid Hills,
Carrick Knowe, Craigentinny,
Silverknowes and Portobello.

Ice Rink
Murrayfield Ice Rink
Open: August-June

Skiing
Hillend Ski Centre, Pentland Hills
Open: Daily 9.30am-9pm, May-August.
Closed 5pm at weekends.
Largest artificial ski slope in Britain.

Sports Centres

The major centres are:
Meadowbank Sports Centre,
139 London Road
Open: Daily 9am-9.30pm.
Cafeteria.

The Royal Commonwealth Pool,
Dalkeith Road
Open: Monday-Friday 9am-9pm,
Saturday-Sunday 8am-7pm.
Sauna suite: Monday-Friday 10am-8pm,
Saturday-Sunday 10am-3pm.
Costume and towel hire available.

Craiglockhart Sports Centre.

GARDENS

Holyrood Park
Laid out around Holyroodhouse.
Extensive views from Arthur's Seat,
Duddingston Loch bird sanctuary.

Princes Street Gardens
Substantial floral displays including
oldest floral clock in the world.

Royal Botanic Garden
Inverleith Road
Gardens Open: Daily, except 25
December and 1 January, 9am-sunset
except Sunday, 11am-sunset.
Plant houses and exhibition hall open:
10am, 11am Sunday, to 5pm approx.
The gardens close 1 hour before sunset
during operation of British Summer
Time.

Saughton Rose Garden
Gorgie Road

ZOOS

Edinburgh Zoo
Corstorphine Road
Tel: 031-334-9171
Open: Daily 9am-6pm (dusk in winter).

FESTIVALS

Edinburgh Festival
22 August-11 September. Brochure and
booking details available from
Edinburgh Festival Society Ltd, 21
Market Street.

Edinburgh Tattoo
Details from Tattoo Manager, 1
Cockburn Street.

Film Festival
Details from The Director, Edinburgh
International Film Festival, 88 Lothian
Road.

Folk Festival
Details from 170 High Street (send
stamps but no envelope).

Royal Highland Show
Ingliston
Third week of June.

TOURIST INFORMATION AND ACCOMMODATION CENTRE

5 Waverley Bridge
Tel: 031-226-6591

Lothian Region Transport,
Waverley Bridge Transport Information
Office
Tel: 031-556-5656
Details of Coach Tours and Touristcard

USEFUL ADDRESSES

Accommodation
The City of Edinburgh Tourist
   Accommodation Service,
9 Cockburn Street,
Edinburgh EH1 1BR
Tel: 031-226-6591

Transport
Lothian Region Transport Enquiries
   Office,
14 Queen Street,
Edinburgh
Tel: 031-554-4494

Scottish Omnibuses,
Bus Station,
St Andrews Square,
Edinburgh
Tel: 031-556-8464

Recreation
The City of Edinburgh Recreation
   Department,
27 York Place,
Edinburgh EH1 3HP
Tel: 031-225-2424

Tattoo
Tattoo Manager,
1 Cockburn Street,
Edinburgh EH1 1QB

Fringe
Fringe Society,
170 High Street,
Edinburgh EH1 1QS

Scottish Borders Tourist Board,
Municipal Buildings,
High Street,
Selkirk
Tel: 0750 20555

Dumfries and Galloway Tourist Board,
District Offices,
Sun Street,
Stranraer
Tel: 0776 2151

The National Trust for Scotland,
5 Charlotte Square,
Edinburgh EH2 4DU

NOTE
While every care has been taken in the
compilation of these pages, it will be
appreciated that opening times and
circumstances can change from time to
time. Please check locally or in local
literature. The author and publishers
would be pleased to hear of any
alterations or amendments.

Index

Going places?

THE
WOODLAND
CENTRE

Enjoy the wonderful world of trees. Three miles north of Jedburgh near the junction of A68/B6400. Woodland walks, slide/tape programmes, giant board games old and new, woodwork exhibits, adventure play area, Natural History bookshop, tearoom.

A place for all the family

Ideal for groups or party visits, outings, conferences

Further information and party bookings:

The Factor, Lothian Estates Office, Jedburgh, Roxburghshire TD8 6UF Tel. Jedburgh 2201

May Scott's
Mill Shop

All garments are made on the premises and available ONLY at May Scott's
Special orders taken and designs discussed with customers.

Ample Parking Facilities
Hours of opening — Monday to Saturday 9.30am to 5.30pm; Sunday 11am to 5.30pm

★ *Exclusive Cashmere Intarsias designed knitwear*
★ *Matching skirts and tops*
★ *Hand-knitted Arran*
★ *Selection of all-wool cloth*
Garments can be made to customer's own specifications and colour.

MAY SCOTT
**1 CABERSTON ROAD
WALKERBURN
PEEBLESHIRE
SCOTLAND**
Or phone (0896-87) 286

Selkirk glass

Visitors Welcome

At our Factory and Showroom to view our range of Hand Made Paperweights and Vases

Monday-Thursday 9am-12.30pm and 1.30pm-5pm Friday 9am-12 noon

Selkirk Glass Limited

Linglie Mill, Riverside Road (on Riverside Industrial Area), Selkirk, Selkirkshire TD7 5EQ.

Tel: Selkirk (0750) 20954

TOURING The
BORDERS?

For all your
Motoring needs
contact —

BORDER MOTOR
COMPANY

Agents For

VOLVO

SALES : SERVICE :
PARTS
BREAKDOWN
SERVICE
**HAVELOCK STREET
HAWICK**
Tel. Hawick
73881

IT'S GREAT OUTDOORS

Open April to October 4 Pennant AA classification RAC appointed. Showers, Toilets, Electric plug-in points, Laundry, Campers, Kitchen, Dish Washing Facilities

Shop, Licensed Bars (with Live Music at Weekends), Basket Suppers in Bars, Take Away Meals.

Garden Centre, Public Telephone, Roller Skating, Bicycles for Hire, Tourist Information, Luxury Caravans for Hire Ideal for Caravans, Tents and Motor Vans

LILLIARDSEDGE —PARK—
JEDBURGH
Telephone: ANCRUM 271

PLANNING A VISIT TO THE SCOTTISH BORDERS?

Contact us for a free accommodation guide from the Tourist Information Centres and visit us in the following towns:

Coldstream	Hawick	Peebles
Eyemouth	Kelso	Selkirk
Galashiels	Melrose	Jedburgh

Open from May-September except Jedburgh which is open throughout the year. All the centres can make local accommodation bookings for you, free of charge. Detailed information about local attractions.

Scottish Borders Tourist Board, Municipal Buildings, High Street, SELKIRK TD7 4JX Tel: (0750) 20555

If you are planning a holiday in the Alps and enjoy walking, whether it be a gentle woodland walk or a more demanding high-level route, then *Walking in the Alps* is a must. There are 112 suggested walks each with their own detailed map, based around 16 different tour centres conveniently arranged for a week's holiday in any one area. Places of interest are also highlighted. Illustrated with colour and black and white photographs, the book is 192 pages long and costs £6.95.

Available from:
**Moorland Publishing Co Ltd
9-11 Station Street,
Ashbourne, Derbyshire
(Tel: 0334 44486)**

STAND UP
AND BE
COUNTED

Drawing by courtesy of Scottish Tourist Board.

8,000 Scots support our work conserving Scotland's threatened Wildlife.

SCOTTISH
WILDLIFE
TRUST

For only £6 a year you can join as an ordinary member. You will receive our Trust Journal ' Scottish Wildlife ', published 3 times a year. But you can also join actively in the work of our many branches throughout the country. Send for details in our colour leaflet.

Send £6 annual subscription or write for details to : —

SM2 Scottish Wildlife Trust,
25 Johnston Terrace,
EDINBURGH EHI 2NH.
Tel: 031-226-4604